CLASSIC

BUS

YEARBOOK 1995

Edited by Gavin Booth

IAN ALLAN Publishing

CONTENTS

First published 1995

ISBN 0 7110 2354 9

Published by Ian Allan Publishing

an imprint of Ian Allan Ltd, Terminal House, Station Approach, Shepperton, Surrey TW17 8AS.
Printed by Ian Allan Printing Ltd, Coombelands House, Coombelands Lane, Addlestone, Weybridge, Surrey KT15 1HY.

INTRODUCTION

When we started *Classic Bus* magazine in 1992 we felt that there was a need for a quality magazine dealing exclusively with older buses and coaches. We put our money where our mouths were, and *CB* has attracted a faithful and growing following among those enthusiasts wishing to indulge in a bi-monthly orgy of downright nostalgia.

This first *Classic Bus Yearbook* is a natural extension of the magazine, and includes the successful mix of articles and photo-features, as well as the quirky items that *CB* readers have come to expect.

From the start we recruited the best writers and photographers for *CB*, and most of the names in this book will be familiar to readers. The doyen of transport journalists, Alan Townsin, contributes a new view of wartime bus operations; Alan Millar takes a critical look at London Transport's apparent loss of direction in the 1970s; Peter Hesketh remembers the buses of Leyland-based independent, Fishwick; Stewart Brown recalls postwar Scottish Albions; T. W. Moore looks back at a once-famous Midland scrapyard; P. R. Wallis illustrates South Wales buses in black-and-white and colour; Michael Dryhurst describes postwar Sussex; Robert E. Jowitt looks back in his characteristic style at British-built buses in Portugal; John G. Lidstone illustrates encounters with boiling buses; Paul Kelly writes on holiday trips to southwest England; and Peter Durham offers classic studies of preserved trolleybuses.

In between, scattered throughout the book, are The Classic Bus Alphabet and a feature on buses and architectural gems.

We hope you enjoy this first *Classic Bus Yearbook* and would remind you that the same mix of articles and photographs can be enjoyed in each bi-monthly issue of *Classic Bus*.

Gavin Booth
Editor

Title page: Manchester Corporation buried some of its trams with Titans like this Leyland-bodied TD1 example, labelled up for the famous 53 route.

Right: The last roofbox RT in London was No RT3062, purchased by Ensign after a long period in store. Returned to service immaculately repainted in Ensignbus yellow and silver with brown trim, it was initially very temperamental in the water department (*see 'One Lump or Two' article P101-105*). A warning cloud of steam blasts along the bonnet, but its driver was determined not to treat his Saunders-bodied steed to a cooling drink.

THE FINALE OF BUSES AND BIRDS

Respected photographer, T. W. MOORE recalls a 1964 visit to Bird's scrapyard at Stratford-on-Avon.

BUSES LAY everywhere, in all forms of cannibalisation; most were unrecognisable hulks that had been here for years. There had been a battle here between the scrapman and the bus... and the bus had lost. This was a graveyard. This was Bird's Commercial Motors of Stratford-on-Avon in Warwickshire, 12 March 1964. Someone once said 'A visit to Bird's would give any bus enthusiast an instant heart attack.'

I must admit that my eager anticipation had turned to shock and disbelief as I surveyed the scene from a concrete shelf fronting this 250sq yd site. Bird's, of course, was one of the leading companies nationwide in the business of scrapping buses and was lethal in its swift action to reclaim the metal salvage for the furnaces and to recover useful running parts for their bus resale activities at home and abroad. What I was seeing was the waste of their pickings, left to rot all over the site, until the time came to clear them out.

My first steps into this graveyard had been down a steep bank to the floor level of the site, up to 80ft deep in parts, through heavy metal waste, old lorries, vans, cars, bits of old buses and many tyres — to a point where 40 or more rotting hulks that were once double-decker buses stretched the whole length of the site before me. Only the muted 'clink-clonk' sound of cutting metal broke the eerie silence as I made my way between the old bodies.

Left: A general view of the Bird's yard at Stratford-on-Avon on 12 March 1964 showing buses stripped of all their useful parts. Most are motorbuses, but there are three-axle trolleybus bodies in the centre of the photograph.
All photographs by T. W. Moore

Top: A Huddersfield Karrier trolleybus with Roe body languishes at Bird's in June 1966.

Above: Still untouched in the summer of 1964, a group of ex-Birmingham Daimler CVD6s await their fate.

Top: This Birmingham Daimler COG5, CVP 157, had lost most of its chassis and most of its Metro-Cammell body in this March 1964 view.

Above: Only the registration plate helps to identify the remains of a 1931 Birmingham AEC Regent at Bird's in March 1964.

Most lay on their sides; some were piled on top of each other extending up the perimeter bank slopes. All I could see had been clinically stripped, discarded and forgotten.

Remnants of red, blue, green and cream paint, on rusting and rotting frames bleached by the seasons, their insides tangled by the twisting bare branches of brambles and elderberry. There was certainly the red of London Transport roofbox RTs and three-axle trolleybuses said to have been scrapped here in the mid-1950s. It was some discoloured maroon paint that led me to the only carcass I could recognise. Its CWK 190 registration plate was the brightest thing on this total wreck of a former Brush-bodied Daimler COA6 from the Coventry Corporation fleet, cocooned here since 1950.

A gem of a find, close by, was the engine and radiator of a former Birmingham City Transport AEC Regent I, OV 4456, lying upside-down. This was a 1931 bus that had run on producer gas during the war in Birmingham, and which had been here since 1950. Its Short 48-seat wooden-framed body lay among the many pieces of bus remains in the nearby undergrowth.

Remains

Other long time residents were body shells from Birmingham Daimler COG5s. Many of these buses ended their days in this scrapyard and their remains could be seen all over the site — in fact, at times I had been completely surrounded by them. I did see CVP 205 and EOG 171 dumped on their sides, the top deck framework of EOG 171 sagged into the ground — but their registration plates shone like new despite the rot surrounding them. The cab front of CVP 174 lay in a mass of BCT bus remains next to the turned-over carcass of COG5 single-decker AOP 56.

The very latest COG5s withdrawn by BCT in 1959/60 were sold to Bird's soon after. Those that remained had been picked and poked, shoved and crushed, rendering them useless.

There was CVP 157, its dulled radiator, engine, bonnet and cab which had been severed from its Metro-Cammell bodywork was nowhere to be seen. CVP 150/155 and COH 915 had been stripped to their bones next to a Birmingham-registered Austin 10 van and a London Transport RT, FXT 233, painted red and cream. CVP 120, another COG5 with an English Electric Manchester-style body that Bird's had sold to Laurie of Hamilton and then returned without being used, had been reduced to a skeleton, following its temporary escape.

The sight of six more of these COG5s shoved over the banked edges of this scrapyard, bared Metro-Cammell frames with some seats still intact and clinging together like old friends, was pitiful to see. CVP 169/184/209 and COX 989 were four of them, and BOP 814, English Electric-bodied, lay half buried underneath them. CVP 127, another Metro-Cammell bus, stood above them on the concrete

Top: The skeleton of one of Birmingham's prewar standard Daimler COG5s sits in the undergrowth in March 1964.

Right: Rescued from Bird's and fully restored, CVP 207, the sole survivor of the Birmingham Daimler COG5s, is pictured at the Sandwell rally in May 1983.

shelf of the site, its cab door flung open to a nesting bird and with tyres flattened on the uneven surface.

Sole survivor

Relief came with CVP 207, which stood complete and untouched, but looking every bit its 23 years of age, parked next to a grubby line of London RTs. When photographing it I had no idea that it was to become the sole surviving Daimler COG5 double-decker from the 800 placed into service with Birmingham. The following July, Barry Ware, a Birmingham bus enthusiast, and his friends had the foresight to purchase it for preservation, and drove that bus out of Birds into safe-keeping. It later became part of the 1685 group's collection and is now part of the display at the Birmingham Museum of Transport at Wythall… and well worth seeing.

Among this apparent Birmingham bus monopoly at Bird's, buses from many fleets were to be seen, like the former prewar Oldham Corporation Leyland TD4, without number and retaining only its front and rear upper panels in its stripped frame. A Stratford Blue and former Midland Red

Above: This 1967 group includes ex-London RTs and ex-Birmingham Daimler CVD6s, as well as the mysterious ex-Stevensons Leyland referred to in the text.

Below: A grubby line of London roofbox RTs seen at Bird's in March 1964.

Below: This is the end of the road for ex-Swindon Daimler CVG5 No 62, a 1947 model with Park Royal body, at Bird's in 1966.

Bottom: An ex-Coventry Daimler CVA6 with Metro-Cammell bodywork acts as a support for an intriguing selection of vehicle remains.

SON, DHA 731, converted some years ago as a treelopper stood on an uphill slope complete, but I did not see this vehicle rolled over at a later date. Two former Cardiff Corporation Bristol K5Gs were in a poor state. One had been savagely decapitated a long time ago, and the other, CKG 581, was lying underneath many Birmingham bus parts with just its rear end showing. A postwar Preston Corporation Leyland PD1/A, BCK 937, which was standing on all wheels and tyres with engine intact, had had its top deck sliced off. One had the impression this vehicle had been used as a tow-and-push bus within the site. A Crossley DD42 from the Baxter of Airdrie fleet was sinking into the ground having sustained a crumpled front mudguard and two smashed windows on its Roe bodywork. Three Swindon Corporation Daimler CVG5s were seen parked so close to the perimeter fencing they looked to be part of it. EMW 898/905/906 were complete. Before leaving the scrapyard on this first visit, I noted that a postwar BCT Daimler had arrived. It was Metro-Cammell-bodied CVA6 GOE 504 new in 1947, and painted red and cream having spent a short time with Superb Coaches of Birmingham. It was the vanguard of what was to follow, for in April 1964, Bird's purchased its last big batch of Birmingham buses, 50 in all, two more CVA6s and 48 CVDs from the 1756-1843 series, HOV 756, etc. All had been ousted by the new Daimler Fleetlines.

I saw those Daimlers in the following summer parked in groups deep down in the scrapyard standing so close to each other you could not slide a hand between them, and despite their well-kept BCT condition, they were destined to go no further. Bird's was selling RTs at the time and these machines had proved such a good second-hand buy, with ample spares to go with them, that the role of the CVDs with their less popular engines had been relegated to one of scrap material only.

By the summer of 1966 and January 1967, the dates of my last visits to the scrapyard, a start had been made in removing registration plates

supplied to Coventry Transport with Metro-Cammell bodies in 1950, had been stripped and dumped, despite the low mileage clocked-up in their 15 years service. One of the CVD6s, GKV 98, lay at an angle on a pile of scrap with two Austin trucks and a Lea Francis car on top of it. FHP 11, a CVA6, had become a burnt-out carcass... how good that bus looked just a few years earlier when I photographed it in the washbay at CCT Sandy Lane depot contrasting so much with this latest picture. And the sight of another CVA6, GVK 91, lying with radiator and engine torn from their mountings in a frozen frosty pool, chilled this 'Coventry Kid' down to the icy ground he was standing on. How I wanted to haul GKV 91's chromed radiator from its icy grave and take it home with me. But, I remembered the ear-bashing, finger-wagging lecture from the scrapyard foreman: 'Don't touch anything. Don't be long. It's at your own risk, and report to me when you leave.' Evidently I had followed in the wake of a group of enthusiasts discovered taking home souvenirs. It was enough to deter me or any enthusiast from taking home any such pieces; the photographs I had taken would have to be my souvenirs.

Above: An October 1969 photo from above the site reveals the remains of prewar and postwar double-deckers.

and radiators with their precious metals.

Keeping the scrapmen busy

More Daimlers from the Coventry Transport fleet and many RTs had arrived for scrapping and the site looked full of buses keeping the scrapmen busy. The Coventry buses, nine Daimler CVA6s, two CVD6s and one CWA6, including three Maudslay Regents all looked too good to scrap, but alas all had taken a bashing. The Maudslays which were among the last nine built at the Maudslay Parkside works in Coventry and

Pockets of red could be seen over the site where the RTs stood, like RT433, HLX 250, a bus I had seen as a sale candidate during my first visit in 1964, but now lying at an angle surrounded by compressed tin cans next to another RT propped up by a wooden stake.

A surprise find on the site were a couple of ex-Huddersfield Corporation Daimler (I think), three-axled trolleybuses, DVH 140 was one. Both had been thrown to the ground next to groups of BCT CVD6s and RTs. Other buses to note were a

Beverley Bar-bodied Guy Arab, GKH 698, from East Yorkshire, painted red and cream, having just lost its rear offside wheels, and two splendid-looking Birkenhead Massey-bodied Leyland PD1s, BG 9231/9233 untouched but deep in the scrapyard.

In 1969, an avalanche of activity saw the scrapmen in full swing. Nothing was spared. Everything had to go, as Bird's took steps to clear the site, transferring all the business in Warwickshire to its site in Long Marston. But it had been said that one bus did escape this rout at Birds. A former Birmingham Leyland TD6c that had been in service with Stevensons of Spath, and which appeared as a black roof among BCT CVDs and RTs in one of my pictures, had literally been clutched from the scrapmen's hammers in part-cannibalised state for intended preservation and which has mysteriously disappeared since. *[Does any reader know if this bus still survives? Ed]*

I can remember pushing my camera through the tall chequered-metal fencing and through leafy branches above the site to photograph the aftermath of the scrapmen's work. It was a sea of destruction — bare herringboned frames and crumpled buses. I'll never forget the groups of BCT CVD6s that had been battered beyond recognition down to their axles where they had stood since 1964, by the swinging weight of the scrapyard crane, with engines, gearboxes seats and panels intact. It was an awful sight. HOV 774/88/94/5/800/2/10/1/4/22/5 were among this carnage. I wondered whether HOV 822 still had its commemorative plaque mounted on its crushed bulkhead, for its visit to the 1948 Trade Fair in Copenhagen as a new bus. More of these CVD6s had been pulled out of their groups and scrapped separately. HOV764/71/84/803/4/12/4/27 were some. HOV 807 lay in fragments of its own waste; its registration plate the only clue to its identity through my camera's telephoto lens.

I stood staring at those CVD6s for some time. I've since read that they were the smoothest and most refined of BCT postwar buses. The gentle roar of their CD6 engines, thirsty perhaps, but a sheer pleasure to hear, and to me the Rolls-Royce sound of any bus engine. It was indeed a sad end.

I never left Bird's without a feeling of sadness. Overcome at times, I had witnessed the finale of the bus, its very last stop and I fully understood that quotation. A visit to Bird's could well give any bus enthusiast an instant heart attack.

T. W. Moore photographs and the occasional article featuring Coventry Transport and bus photography have appeared in bus magazines and books since the late 1950s. A busy press photographer for some 39 years, Tom combines his bus photography hobby with breeding fancy goldfish at his Coventry home.

Left: Birmingham, Coventry and London buses pictured in their final resting-place in October 1969.

Classic Bus Alphabet/1

A IS FOR INITIALS — well, not really, but if you want to be first in your local Yellow Pages choose a name starting with A. In bus terms if you want to be first in the Coach Hire section you could call yourself Aardvark Coaches. Until early in 1995 Ayrshire boasted two companies vying for alphabetic supremacy — AA Buses and A1 Service, both named long before your fingers were expected to do the walking. These were originally groups of independents, co-operatives to fight the might of the territorial bus companies, and were good easy-to-remember names unless you were a dyslexic, colour-blind passenger living in Ardrossan or Irvine where both AA and A1 operated. Other A initials include ACB (one-time Sunderland coachbuilder); various London bus garage codes including the logical AG (Ash Grove) and less obvious (it's a long story) AF (Putney); and AN (vastly-improved Leyland Atlantean).

B IS FOR BLAKEY, Stephen Lewis's officious moustached inspector in television's On the Buses. His 'Get that bus out!' catchphrase caught the nation's imagination a quarter of a century ago in the days before two-way radios, route tracking, Wayfarer ticket machines and other technological wonders turned him into an endangered species. Less lamented than the clippie, the inspector played a vital role in checking for fares evasion, late or early running and in organising the efficient despatch of buses from their depots, yet we best remember him (or her) as a real-life Blakey for whom everything — especially satisfying the customer — was too much trouble.

C IS FOR CLASSIC. It's an overworked word. Classic Bus. Classic car. Classic this. Classic that. When it should mean something just a bit special ('of the first class, of acknowledged excellence, outstandingly important' says The Concise Oxford Dictionary) it is now commonly nothing more than a big word for old.
Some old buses are classics. The RT comes to

Above: A classic bus, certainly: the Bristol Lodekka — though hardly helped by the lack of a grille on this 1958 Crosville LDS flat-floor prototype. The grille was rendered superfluous by the Cave-Brown-Cave heating system, whose grilles were on either side of the destination display, but subsequent Lodekkas carried a 'proper' grille after all.

mind. It epitomises all that was good in British bus design in the final years of the 1930s. Its four-bay body construction was trend-setting.
Or the Bristol Lodekka. It adopted a workable engineering solution to the problem of buses and bridges. It was surely a classic.
But can the same be said of, for example, a Leyland Titan PD1 with its rasping 7.4-litre engine? It's old, yes. But was it an advance on the TD7?
Or am I simply in danger of redefining the word 'classic' to serve my own needs?

D IS FOR DENNIS — 100 years old this year, but it is only in the last few years that Dennis has really risen to the ascendancy in the bus world. Indeed from 1968, in which year it built two complete buses for Llandudno UDC on Pax V chassis (which barely counted as buses!), until 1977, when it launched the Dominator, it built not a single bus. Indeed in the years up to 1968, its output flagged somewhat, with penny numbers of Lolines after its last big effort, 28 Lolines for Aldershot & District in 1965. Indeed one could well wonder what would have become of Dennis

Left: The first batch of Dennis Loline III leaving the Dennis works for Falkirk where they would receive Alexander bodies. The customer? You guessed — Aldershot & Distrct.

without Aldershot & District, who ran buses past its factory and therefore possibly felt obliged to buy them.

Would it have survived to be the flourishing bus manufacturer it is today? Indeed if one had rattled up Great Orme on one of Llandudno UDC's Pax Vs in 1968, could one have predicted that Dennis would be Britain's only British-owned bus chassis manufacturer within 25 years?

Dennis was well-known for turning out rarities, and is reported to have been very embarrassed in the 1950s when it set up a production line (please whisper it!), albeit to build ambulances.

Traditional Dennis customers included Aldershot & District, Walsall Corporation, East Kent (with some splendid Lancet UF coaches amongst other single-deckers), Aldershot & District, Southdown, Lancashire United, Aldershot & District, West Bromwich, Merthyr Tydfil, Aldershot & District, Singapore Traction, Bowens, Jersey Motor Traction, Western Australia Government Transport, Kowloon Motor Bus — oh, and Aldershot & District. However when it started building Bristol Lodekkas under licence it did rather better; indeed it went mad and built over 280 of them, for a wide range of customers — but most of them for, well yes, you've guessed — Aldershot & District! Things changed after 1977 — for a start there was no such thing as Aldershot & District, but by then we had got beyond things classic, so we'll wait a few years before getting all nostalgic about Darts.

E IS FOR EASTERN. Bus operators have always been fairly pedantic over company names. So if you start up a bus company in East Anglia, what do you call it? Eastern Counties, actually, not to be confused with its southern neighbour, Eastern National. Scottish Omnibuses had been called SMT, but when somebody realised that this was geographically inaccurate, the company became Eastern Scottish. The passengers still called it SMT.

Other Easterns include Eastern Coach Works, a spin-off from Eastern Counties; and Eastern Belle, a well-known London area independent. Then there were the 'Easts' — Kent, Lancs, London, Midland, as well as two appearances in Selnec (South East Lancashire North East Cheshire). Imaginative, or what?

F IS FOR FROG, the industry's nickname for the equivalent of points on a trolleybus system's overhead wiring. Don't ask why (although you may be able to tell us) but we guess it's got something to do with it leaping from one route to another. (See also P76).

G IS FOR GLASGOW CORPORATION TRANSPORT, widely acknowledged to be Europe's most efficient public transport system. In the late 1930s it offered low fares and ran a modern fleet of buses and an even more modern fleet of trams.

At least, that's the perceived wisdom. Its efficiency doesn't seem to be in question, although its modernity might well be challenged. The impressive new trams of the 1930s and 1940s were rubbing shoulders with outdated Edwardian cars almost until the system closed in 1962.

There were trolleybuses too, but the Glaswegian's fondness for his municipal transport system declined as the tramway network contracted and trolleybuses ('the silent death') and motorbuses took over.

It wasn't simply cause and effect. In the heady days of the 1950s and 1960s staff shortages and high staff turnover led to a decline in service standards. Some would say they've never recovered.

IT WASN'T ALL DOOM AND GLOOM

ALAN TOWNSIN recalls some of the brighter aspects of the bus scene during the 1939-45 war

NATURALLY, and quite rightly, war is seen as a catastrophic event, and pictures from the former Yugoslavia on our television screens have emphasised how normal life is often turned into tragedy. Yet even amid the death and destruction, there were brighter moments as well as valuable lessons for the bus industry.

Knowledge of what had happened in Spain, China and Ethiopia in the 1930s caused expectations of heavy air raids and massive casualties, leading to much emphasis on air raid precautions, or ARP as it was called, in the early stages. Some 400 Green Line coaches were converted very quickly into ambulances under a pre-arranged scheme when the services on which they ran were withdrawn on 1 September 1939, and that same day, I found myself an 'evacuee', being transported with the rest of my school from Newcastle-on-Tyne to Penrith. Similar activities occurred all over the country. Two days later, Britain was officially at war.

Yet once there, the bus scene was to remain one of the more reassuring reflections of relative normality, apart from the white-painted mudguard edges and dim lighting, and much the same applied elsewhere. Services were cut to save fuel, and many operators painted roof panels grey or other unobtrusive colours to make them less

Right: Public transport was in the front line when air raids on British cities began in earnest in the latter part of 1940. This was the scene in Sheffield's High Street on 12 December that year, with one of the Corporation's trams almost reduced to ashes and two more in danger of following suit as buildings blaze nearby. Fire brigades were largely overwhelmed by the numbers of fires started in such attacks. Tram systems were often crippled — part of the overhead wiring visible here has collapsed — but Sheffield managed to get its system going again, some services running two days later through it took about two months to get the whole system back into use. Eleven trams were burnt out and 20 more badly damaged, though most of the latter were repaired.
Alan Townsin collection

Above: The outbreak of war caused the shelving of a number of projects for new models. One that suffered this fate was recorded in Leyland records as an LS1. It was completed in December 1940 and apparently intended to be a new single-deck model, with the L-type 6.2 litre six-cylinder engine which had been fitted to some Ribble Leyland Tiger TS8 models in 1939, possibly as a successor to the prewar Lion LT and/or Cheetah LZ series. It was supplied to Lincolnshire Road Car and is seen here in Newark. As was often the case in eastern and southern England, the normal dark green and cream livery of this operator was quite extensively modified to reduce visibility from the air, though in this case the lower panels appear to be in standard green.
G. H. F. Atkins

conspicuous from the air. Yet there were even some new buses, if not as many as usual, still entering service in many fleets and, contrary to a widespread impression, there was at first no sign of austerity about them — indeed, many were superior to their predecessors, sometimes notably so. To some degree, this was simply the 'pipeline' effect, in that work in hand was completed.

Perhaps most notably, delivery from AEC of the chassis for London Transport's first 150 production RT-type buses did not begin until October 1939, the first few entering service in January 1940. Leyland announced a new version of the Titan, the TD7, also in October 1939, and over 300 were ordered and built in the normal way, entering service with operators in many parts of Britain in the period up to 1941. All of these had bodywork to full peacetime standards — indeed many were clearly an advance on what had gone before — and the same was true of double and single-deck buses in general of this period, largely on AEC, Bristol, Daimler and Leyland chassis. A small proportion of these vehicles were not delivered to their intended recipients but were soon found new homes.

Although non-essential services were curtailed, the need to get workers to factories meant that many fleets in industrial areas were soon at full stretch.

Military production

Many bus manufacturers were quite busy with military production of one kind or another even before the war began, as there had been a gradual build-up over the previous year or two, and some dropped civilian production altogether, almost immediately. Yet bus output continued in most cases more or less undisturbed even if at a slower rate than usual.

Then the threat of invasion, as the German armies swept through the Low Countries and France fell in 1940, put the whole country on an emergency footing. Bus output largely stopped, save for completion of part-built vehicles, and even that was often delayed as parts or materials became scarce or unobtainable. The Eastern Coach Works premises at Lowestoft were shut at a day's notice in May when invasion was seen as an imminent risk, and Daimler output was brought to a stop by severe air raid damage, mainly during the 11-hour raid of 14 November 1940, though both firms were able to restart later, in temporary premises. Air raids, often by quite large numbers of Luftwaffe bombers, were suffered by London and many industrial cities, in 1940-41 particularly. The south coast was an obvious target and at Dover, East Kent's local bus services were within range of German guns until 1944.

All this was horrific and quite a number of bus operators suffered, and numbers of staff as well as passengers, were killed or injured. There were several instances of bus garages being severely

Below: Prototypes for postwar models brought a gleam of hope amid the wartime gloom, and RT19 was possibly the most effective and influential of these. Within a few weeks of entering service with London Transport in January 1940, it returned to AEC and embarked on a career as both development prototype and demonstrator which continued intermittently through much of the war. Its specification became the basis of not only the postwar London RT fleet but in major mechanical features, that of the standard Regent and Regal MkIII as sold generally, collecting many orders in the wake of its travels. Here it is seen in the green demonstrator livery it carried for a time, based on that of Mansfield District, while operating for Nottingham City Transport in September 1940. The RT's low radiator was copied by Bristol, Crossley and Guy on their postwar models, but not adopted, oddly enough, by AEC itself for its own standard range. G. H. F. Atkins

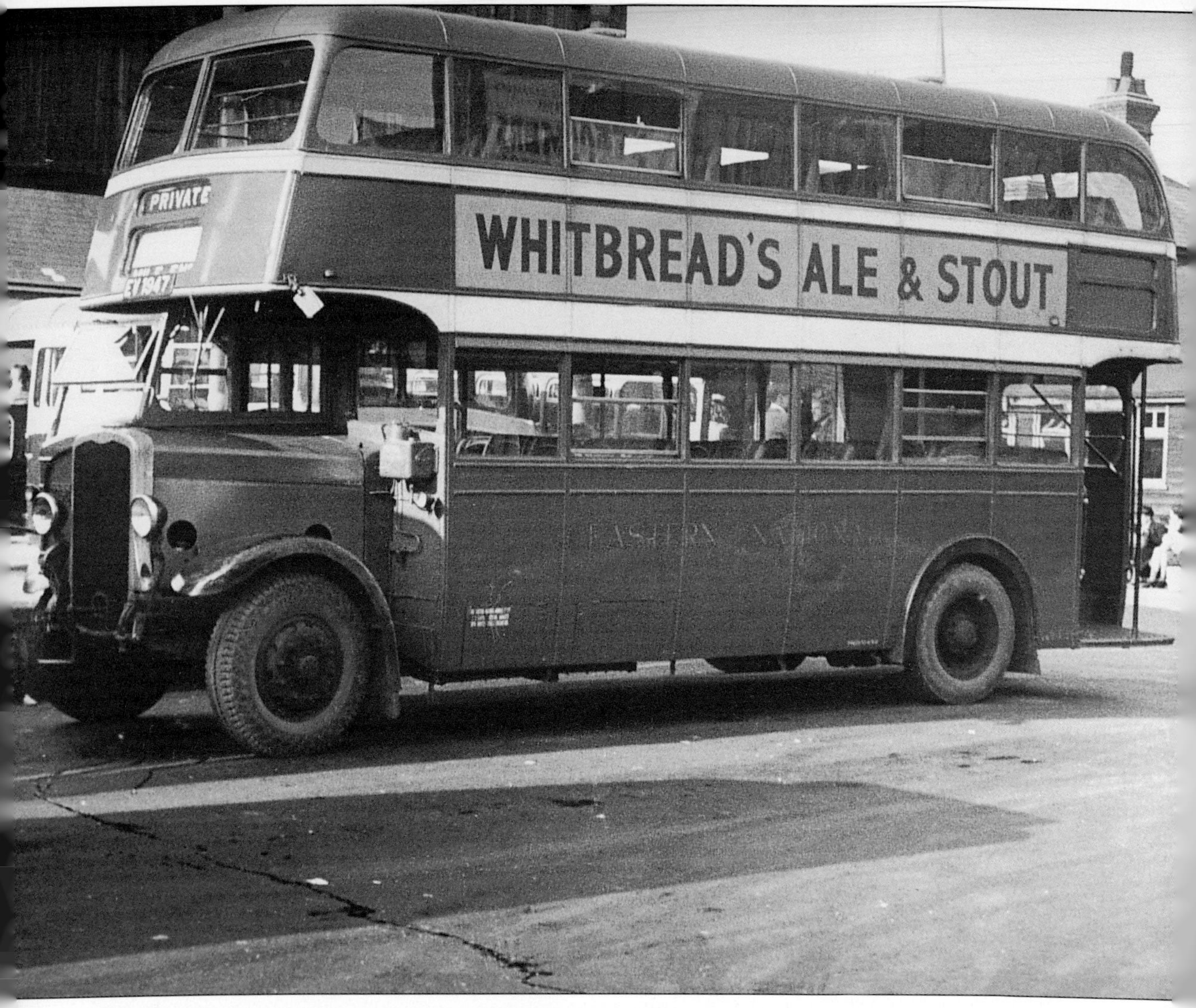

Above: The war encouraged an increase in rebodying of existing chassis, sometimes with strange results. At a quick glance, this Eastern National double-decker looked like a standard Bristol K5G with ECW body as built for various Tilling fleets from 1937. That it was something very different became obvious when it moved off, for it sounded just like a petrol-engined Leyland Titan TD1 of the 1928-31 period. In fact, it was neither, being a Thornycroft XC, a rare interim model, of 1931, to which a Leyland engine and gearbox had been fitted at an unknown date, and rebodied by ECW in 1941. It is not known whether the Bristol radiator may have been a later addition, not an uncommon ploy to disguise old buses in Tilling fleets. This photograph was taken at Colchester in 1948.
Alan Townsin

damaged by direct hits, sometimes with numerous buses damaged or destroyed, in addition to those hit while on the road, though thankfully passengers and crews were at least sometimes in the air raid shelters found in urban areas. Tramway systems due for replacement were generally reprieved, largely because the electric power on which they relied was produced from British coal, unlike motor vehicles which needed fuel which was all imported in those days. However, air raids brought some systems to a premature end, notably at Coventry where the November 1940 raid made tram operation unworkable, as well as damaging over half the bus fleet. At Bristol, air raids in January and April 1941 similarly closed the tram system.

Yet buses proved remarkably hard to kill, and even apparent write-offs often proved capable of being rebuilt, usually with new bodywork. There was a general mood of making do by repair which covered almost every aspect of life, and buses which would have been withdrawn around 1940 survived for far longer. Britain was lucky in that most of the models in service in 1939 were durable in basic design, going back to such types as the Leyland Titan TD1 of 1928-31. Fortunately, this applied particularly to the various makes of double-decker bus and trolleybus which had been placed in service in city fleets in large numbers in the late 1930s, often in the earlier stages of tram replacement programmes. Most of the buses had efficient and reliable diesel engines and many had the benefit of sturdy bodywork, often metal-framed, which would survive even the inevitable wartime neglect without taking too much harm.

Unfrozen and utility

However, it was probably the loss from service of quite substantial numbers of buses in air raids, even though many were eventually repaired or rebodied, that led to the restoration of at least a limited supply of new buses; at first the so-called 'unfrozen' models made from parts in stock and then the 'utility' buses. The latter formed part of a national scheme covering items such as clothing and even furniture, and for a time there seemed to be a deliberate policy of emphasising the austere

Below: The 'unfrozen' vehicles released in 1941/42 were welcomed in fleets sorely in need of new vehicles because of wartime problems but their allocation produced some odd effects. The Hull municipal fleet then standardised on AEC buses but among its allocation were four Leyland Titan TD7 models with Leyland bodywork, the latter intended for Western SMT and having that operator's style of destination box. The TD7 incorporated a heavy flywheel as part of its anti-vibration package, making gear changes slow, and this caused the model to be unpopular with some drivers on urban routes, but was superbly refined. In this view, No 203 (GKH 384) is in grey (in this case with glossy finish, by no means always so), with no reference to the operator's identity and hence the locality; as was common when invasion by German paratroops was a real possibility.
Alan Townsin Collection

Above: Not as bad as expected — the author's first ride in a utility Guy Arab was in one of the small number supplied to United Automobile Services Ltd, proving to be less rough-running than the same fleet's standard peacetime Bristol buses with the same Gardner 5LW engine. Seen here soon after the war, repainted into standard red and cream, is No GD02 (GHN 322) with Roe lowbridge bodywork.
R. A. Mills

aspects. To someone interested in buses, the prospect of what sounded as if they were to be rough-running box-like vehicles was depressing.

Yet I recall very clearly my first ride in a utility Guy Arab, one allocated to United Automobile Services Ltd in 1942, and discovering that it actually was rather less noisy and rough than the same operator's standard Bristol buses having the same Gardner 5LW engine, even if the seats were rather upright and thinly upholstered — the slatted wooden seats did not appear in utility double-deckers until the 1943/44 period. And even the utility bodywork's usual interior finish, the woodwork simply given a coat of light varnish, was not unattractive even if most of them entered service in the grey external paint in which many were delivered, the actual shade varying somewhat according to the bodybuilder. The threat of boring standardisation receded when it was realised that — given very little practice — each bodybuilder had its own interpretation of the utility specification; identifiable on sight.

The only single-decker on offer was the Bedford OWB with standard utility body designed and largely built by Duple (though some were built to the same pattern by Roe, SMT and Mulliner), always supplied in plain brown paintwork, and this did have very cramped wooden seats for 32 passengers. Yet it too had its virtues, such as its smooth petrol engine. Nowadays, it would be counted as a midibus but it wasn't what most big operators wanted then. There was also a utility

Above: The saving grace of the wartime utility buses from the point of view of the contemporary enthusiast was the variety of bodywork. In this line-up of five Derby Corporation Guy Arab I models, the two outer examples, which dated from November 1942, had bodies by Massey Bros of Wigan, a concern whose products became much more widely known due to the war and whose interpretation of the utility specification was very distinctive, if controversial. The middle three, supplied three months later, were bodied by Park Royal, the largest builder of wartime double-deckers, but neither of these concerns had supplied Derby previously — operators had virtually no ability to influence choice of bodywork and at the time these buses were supplied, there was no other make of double-deck bus chassis available. 'Derby' had been omitted from the fleetname.
Alan Townsin Collection

trolleybus, the W-type two-axle model rather surprisingly 'badge-engineered' as either a Karrier or Sunbeam, though it was more truly the latter — the two makes had come under the same ownership prewar.

Pleasing combination

The breadth of choice did widen a little after 1943, when Daimler, and then later Bristol came back into production. The Daimler CWG5 being just as 'civilised' to ride in as the prewar equivalent COG5, with effective flexible mounting of the 5LW engine, fluid flywheel and preselective gearbox. There were only 100 of them, and then came the CWA6, with AEC 7.7-litre six-cylinder engine, admittedly bolted into the frame, so fairly noisy within, but lively, with quite a pleasing combination of sound effects. These observations were also true of the wartime Bristol, the K6A, also AEC-powered, which was sufficiently quieter than the prewar K5G with 5LW to reveal that the Bristol crash gearbox made rather a 'mellow' sound.

But overall, a good deal of the fascination of the wartime breed of bus was the bodywork. A few major firms familiar in prewar days did not take part because of war work, notably Metro-Cammell and English Electric, the latter never to return to buses. But when one lists the main makes that did participate, there was no lack of variety, especially as the allocations made with negligible operator choice by the Ministry of War Transport, spread most all over the country. There were double-deckers on new chassis by Brush, Duple, Massey, Northern Counties, Park Royal, Pickering, Roe, Strachans and Weymann, plus, concentrating mainly on rebodying, Alexander, Beadle, Eastern Coach Works, East Lancashire, Northern Coachbuilders and Willowbrook. Rebodying of single-deckers was largely in the hands of Burlingham, with smaller numbers from Willowbrook.

By about 1941/42, losses of shipping due to submarine attack were becoming a major worry, and there was a fear that fuel would become very scarce, resulting in a directive that all major bus operators were to convert 10% of their fleets to producer gas operation, partly with the idea that wider conversions could follow if need be. This operation was never achieved, but for a time the sight of buses with gas trailers became familiar. The Tilling companies persevered more than most, often converting the more powerful petrol models such as Leyland Tiger or AEC Regal with fair success, but the loss of power and amount of trouble meant that operators gave them up with a

Below: Many buses were painted in a flat grey in wartime, the lack of varnish soon causing ugly stains where fuel was spilt and drivers' hands touched the cab door. Cardiff Corporation No 169 was a 1937 AEC Regent with Northern Counties body of that builder's characteristic style of the period.
Alan Townsin Collection

Above: A rather surprising perhaps, yet rather cheering, element in the wartime scene in various parts of the country was the appearance of London Transport ST-type AEC Regent buses, generally in traditional livery save for the red oxide roof, on quite long periods of loan to a variety of operators as the London situation eased. Here No ST237, originally placed in service by the London General Omnibus Co in 1930, is seen running for Lincolnshire, who operated it from October 1942 to January 1945. It was generally on the Grantham-Nottingham route, being seen in the latter city. Note the crudely boarded-up upper-deck windows — coping with broken glass was a considerable problem. The lower deck window alongside the straight staircase was replaced by a panel on all vehicles of this type, apparently to provide a supply of replacements, and was never restored, even when peace returned.
G. H. F. Atkins

sigh of relief once this was permitted as fuel supplies improved by 1944.

Another reflection of wartime shortages, which pervaded many aspects of life, was the widespread adoption of grey, or other subdued colours, often unvarnished, for repainting buses generally, from about 1941/42. This was largely due to a shortage of pigment, though some operators in the more vulnerable areas had already adopted such schemes, sometimes to replace the normal cream or white relief as a mild form of camouflage against air attack. The actual shades varied considerably between fleets, and passengers grew adept at identifying their bus, even though fleetnames were also sometimes deleted when the names were thought to be of value to an invading army. Fleets varied considerably in this — some with good stocks of their normal colours managed to carry on as usual,

Above: Operators often pressed coaches, redundant from express services shut down to save fuel, into service on bus duties during wartime, and Midland Red modified its SOS LRR-class coaches of 1933-35 to seat 34 instead of 30, repainting them in bus livery in 1940/41 as seen here. These were strange-looking vehicles, the 'L' referring to the low build and 'RR' to the Rolls-Royce-like qualities claimed for the six-cylinder petrol engines, certainly smooth-running, but actually side-valve 6.4 litre units made, like the whole chassis, by the operator. The body, also of Midland Red design, was built by Short Bros.
Alan Townsin Collection

and I recall Rochdale Corporation putting even their wartime buses into the quite elaborate blue and cream livery soon after delivery.

Others simply didn't paint as often, and the only Ribble buses I saw in grey in the northern parts of its territory were those with utility bodywork yet, at least in the Lake District, appearance standards remained quite high in those days of washing by hand. On the other side of the Pennines, things were different, and the United fleet was virtually all in a plain khaki-grey shade by about 1942/43, though matters were improved when a gloss finish was adopted, again quite quickly, thereafter. One or two of the Yorkshire municipal fleets remained largely in grey until a year or so after the war.

Postwar prototypes

In those days, we all lived on hope of better times — the 'sunlit uplands' to which Winston Churchill referred in one of his famous wartime speeches. In the world of buses, very limited work on postwar prototypes was permitted, and a handful of vehicles were completed for development or demonstration purposes.

Among them was London Transport's RT19, borrowed back by AEC, spending spells both at Southall and, painted green, visiting operators in many parts of Britain drumming up business for what had become known as the Regent Mark III. In the process it eventually emerged with a specification which was the basis of the postwar

Above: The war prolonged the lives of many buses. This AEC Regent with Hall Lewis open-staircase body placed in service in January 1930 had been the oldest double-decker in the Newcastle Corporation fleet when war broke out. Due for early withdrawal, being among very few open-stair buses remaining in the area, it remained in service, being one of several which were lent to London Transport to help cope with the dark days of 1940/41. This photograph was taken a few weeks after the end of the war in 1945, with mudguards still edged in white. The paintwork was still in prewar fully lined-out style, probably dating from 1939 or earlier, except for the grey roof, and various minor dents are evident but overall it was quite presentable, bearing in mind all the problems of the times. It was withdrawn from passenger service a few months later but was retained as a service vehicle, latterly a tower wagon, until 1950.
Alan Townsin

fleet of 4,674 RT buses supplied to London Transport.

Bristol made a pair of K5G double-deckers, with chassis outwardly only slightly different to the prewar model as built since 1937, but transformed from the passengers' viewpoint by the adoption of effective flexible engine mountings, sadly not adopted as standard until 1948/49. They received ECW bodywork of design based on that firm's style as being built on a small scale for rebodying purposes, among the least austere of wartime styles and very close to the postwar standard. One was highbridge and went to the Western National fleet, registered JTA 271, while the lowbridge one went to Eastern National as JVW 430.

Crossley built a new prototype double-decker known as type DD42; Manchester Corporation placing it in service in 1944. It had a new design of 8.6-litre engine and torque-converter transmission, and Crossley regained a substantial share of the early postwar bus market on the basis of the new design. Dennis had concentrated on four-cylinder buses since the mid 1930s but built prototype six-cylinder diesel engines in 1940, two going into Lance double-deckers for Walsall Corporation. A prototype single-decker was supplied to Aldershot & District early in 1945 and was the basis of the postwar Lancet III model, with the smooth-running Dennis 06 engine.

Perhaps most adventurous of all, and as more fully described in Classic Bus No 1, Midland Red produced a whole series of prototypes for postwar production of its own-make chassis by then generally known by the initials BMMO of the company's then full title, the Birmingham & Midland Motor Omnibus Co Ltd. Four were single-deckers, produced by converting prewar rear-engined models never put into production. As rebuilt, they were mid-underfloor-engined layout with entrance position ahead of the front axle, a combination unknown in Britain at that date, but its success may be judged, not only by that operator's standardisation on the layout for all its postwar single-deckers, but by almost complete adoption of this layout for full-sized single-deckers in Britain about five years later.

As if that wasn't enough, one new BMMO double-decker was also built in 1944, and although generally orthodox in layout, with front engine and rear entrance, it had a new full-width bonnet design with the radiator concealed, again proving a trend-setter for styles widely adopted from 1950 onwards.

New engines

Other chassis makers had been working on oil engines of their own. Bristol had developed a six-cylinder engine, of which one was running in a United K by about 1944, and proved to give lively and smooth performance on quite a hilly route out of Newcastle — production of the K6B model as an option to K5G or K6A began in 1946. Daimler's engine went into limited production early in 1945, the resulting CWD6 chassis being slotted in among CWA6 models.

Leyland had a new passenger model with 6.2-litre engine under development at the beginning of the war, but was too heavily engaged in war work from 1942 to pursue the project. A clue to future intentions derived from this work came late in 1944 when details of a new 7.4-litre engine then being used in military Hippo six-wheel goods models were released. It was not until just after the war ended that it was announced that it was being incorporated in the new PD1 version of the Titan double-decker then going into production.

Even before the war ended, the worst of wartime restrictions were relaxed, notably in bodywork, with permission to revert to domed outlines for front and rear roof panels and upholstered seats being granted in the autumn of 1944, though the changes were not applied in some cases until well into 1945 and by no means consistently.

In March 1945, it was announced that production of AEC and Crossley double-decker chassis was to be resumed later in the year. The war in Europe ended in May 1945 and Albion single-deck production was added to the list in June. At the beginning of August 1945 a list of makers of double and single-deck chassis (heavy) to be available in 1946 comprised AEC, Albion, BMMO, Bristol, Crossley, Daimler, Dennis, Foden, Guy, Leyland, Thornycroft and Tilling-Stevens, with Maudslay as a 'heavy' coach maker, and Bedford and Commer for light passenger models.

A few days later, the war ended with the surrender of Japan, and the prospect of normality came nearer, though in fact wartime methods and consequences lingered on well into 1946 and although the postwar period was indeed a golden age for buses in many ways, by no means all the wartime hopes and expectations were fulfilled. But it is a sobering thought that, although the new bus supply position in 1942-45 was then thought very meagre, more buses seating 32 or more were added to British fleets in those hard-pressed days than in 1990-3.

Alan Townsin, best remembered by many as one-time editor of Buses Illustrated, has worked on a number of transport journals, and is currently involved in freelance writing.

Above: The splendid glass and iron structure of Durham bus station with British Electric Traction magnet on high, seen in 1966. The station, built in 1928 and one of the first in the country, was demolished in an act of supreme vandalism and the bus station now hides behind a parade of shops. It is thought that the frontage was rescued for the Beamish museum. Robert E. Jowitt

Left: We don't know how often the royal family actually used bus services in Windsor, but until recently they certainly had every opportunity to do so. The Great Western Railway's Windsor & Eton station was built literally across the road from Windsor Castle and incorporated a Royal Station. In time, the station forecourt became the terminus for Thames Valley country bus services as well as the White Bus Service to Ascot. Seen here underneath the imposing portal on 31 May 1971 is Thames Valley No D46, an ECW-bodied Bristol FLF Lodekka. In 1983, recognising the tourist potential, Madame Tussaud's invested £2 million to turn the Royal Station into a representation of the scene there on Queen Victoria's jubilee day in 1897. The buses were ousted to street termini.
P. R. Wallis

SECOND FIDDLE/1

Classic Bus Alphabet/2

H IS FOR HIGHBRIDGE. Highbridge buses were buses which were too high to get under low bridges. Well, up to a point. If however you are the PSV Circle, H is for highbridge, even if highbridge is lowbridge in terms of height. And as the PSV Circle leads the way in the nomenclature for body types, any double-decker these days is H for Highbridge, even if it's low enough to get under bridges too low for a highbridge bus.

You see, like many things, once upon a time life was simple. A double-decker bus was a double-decker bus. Then came Leyland with the Titan TD1. Up until then a lot of double-deckers had been too high to have a roof, because the authorities were frightened they might tip over. The Titan was revolutionary in that it had a low chassis frame and by sinking the upstairs gangway along one side of the bus it could get under low bridges. Thus was born the lowbridge bus (see L). But you could also have a Hybridge version, as Leyland called it, if you didn't have low bridges with which to contend, with a centre gangway upstairs. And it was still low enough to have a roof without falling over.

All well and good. And so things remained for 20 years, until Bristol invented the Lodekka, which made the chassis even lower and used a drop-centre rear axle so that you could have a conventional layout within a lowbridge height. The days of the lowbridge double-decker were numbered (though it was nearly another 20 years before the last was built). But all these new-fangled lowheight models were considered to be highbridge, not because they were higher than lowbridge but because of their seating layout. Nothing in life is simple any more …

I IS FOR IAN ALLAN. Crawling? Well, maybe. But Ian Allan, personally and corporately, attracted many thousands of 'spotters' (horrid word) into the mysteries of trains and buses. It was Ian Allan who, in 1949, created *Buses Illustrated*, a magazine many of us grew up with, which led to its current incarnation as *Buses*. And of course Ian Allan's *Buses Extra* was reborn as *Classic Bus*.

J IS FOR JENSEN or 'JNSN' as the punched metal concealed radiator pressings used to say on this short-lived coach. Possibly the only bus ever produced in West Bromwich, the Jensen was a 40-seat Perkins-engined aluminium integral built between 1948 and 1952. Aluminium made it much more expensive than rival products, but its light weight made it cheap to run. It was derived from a van developed to beat some nonsensical speed and weight restrictions for goods vehicles. When those restrictions ended, Jensen's market disappeared and in its latter years the company concentrated on making the sports cars for which it is most fondly remembered.

K IS FOR KREST. Well, Silver Krest actually. Silver Krest Koaches. It was a pretty dodgy-looking outfit, as you might expect from a company using Ks instead of Cs. But presumably it seemed katchy at the start of the swinging sixties.

Based in Castlemilk on the south side of Glasgow it ran a motley collection of ex-Ribble buses, generally bought from Millburn Motors, a major second-hand dealer. Through Silver Krest Koaches it was possible to chart the up-dating of the Ribble fleet.

Prewar TS7 Tigers with postwar Duple bodies were followed by CCK-registered PD2s and then, as modernity thrust itself north, all-Leyland Royal Tigers.

To be fair to Silver Krest Koaches, they did run a couple of modern vehicles too — Thames Traders (they weren't called Fords then) with attractive Burlingham Seagull '60 bodies — long-forgotten klassics?

L IS FOR LOWBRIDGE (see also H, which is for Highbridge). A lowbridge bus could get under low bridges, so long as they weren't too low, in which case you needed a single-decker. In exceptional circumstances, like Dunham Massey on North Western's 98 service from Altrincham to Warrington, you might need lowbridge single-deckers, though only in more recent times; its Bristol Ls (and here L had nothing to do with Lowbridge) would fit anyway.

The Lowbridge concept was really invented by Leyland with the Titan, and comprised a sunken

Above: A lowbridge single-decker, one of the special Strachan-bodied Bedford VALs bought by North Western in 1964 emerging from the bridge beneath the Bridgewater Canal at Dunham Massey that dictated the unique roof shape. A. Moyes

gangway on the upper deck with awkward rows of four seats and a big bulge into the lower saloon ceiling, giving rise to little notices on the seat backs saying 'Please lower your head when leaving your seat', which most quaint olde worlde pubs with beams and things have now commuted to 'Duck or Grouse', but that would have been a bit frivolous for the starchy bus industry and even starchier Traffic Commissioners in the lowbridge days.

The concept was rendered obsolescent by the Bristol Lodekka in 1949 (see H for Highbridge) though it took until 1968 for the concept to die out; Caerphilly took the last one, as it happens, on another Leyland Titan, in 1968, 40 years after the first one, and that was withdrawn from service by Stevensons of Uttoxeter only in 1994.
Lowbridge buses had a certain quaintness, if you didn't use them every day; if you did, they were a thundering nuisance, as they were difficult to see out of and difficult to get out of. Barton went one stage further by building a lowbridge body on a lowheight chassis, a Dennis Loline, and built the lowest double-decker ever. When Daimler retaliated to Leyland's Atlantean with the Fleetline it sensibly went for a low-height arrangement so Leyland made a lowbridge Atlantean available with a lowbridge arrangement just at the back end, which was very odd. MCW built a body for it where the seats at the rear upstairs were too high to see out of the windows and the seats at the front were too low to see out of the windows. The lowbridge bus was another great British compromise.

M IS FOR MANCUNIAN, not a person but a bus — lots of buses, actually. The idea of naming buses after towns and cities is not that rare. Leyland's frugal Tiger Cub was the Albion Aberdonian. Guy's Wulfrunian was named after a native of Wolverhampton, where this none-too-successful chassis was built. And a half-hearted attempt was made to call the London Transport Daimler Fleetlines 'Londoners'; people just called them DMSs, usually with a hint of cynicism. But both generations of Mancunians were rather more successful. The first lot were prewar Crossley chassis, named doubtless with a prominent customer in mind, and the second lot were the trend-setting one-man double-deckers that Manchester City Transport developed in the late 1960s.

Above: The clean, trend-setting lines of the Mancunian body design, introduced in 1968 for one-person operation with Manchester City Transport. Mounted on Daimler Fleetline and Leyland Atlantean chassis, similar bodies were built by East Lancs, MCW and, as here, Park Royal.

N IS FOR NOTICES. At its best, the bus industry communicates splendidly with its customers (eg London Transport's long tradition of well-thought-out publicity), but its best hasn't always seen the light of day. This Glasgow Corporation announcement of a service withdrawal (right) contains not a whiff of apology and has been plastered carelessly across two completely unrelated and obviously out-of-date notices and doesn't bother to tell you how to find the new bus stop. At least it's spelt properly.

O IS FOR OVERSEAS — it used to be the place where traditional British buses sold in vast numbers. Albions to Australia, AECs to Argentina. Wherever you looked Britain's manufacturers were exporting.

Leyland built uprated versions of its Tiger and Titan — the OPS and OPD series — and sold them far and wide.

British-style double-deckers ran in healthy numbers in Hong Kong, Portugal, South Africa, Kenya, Uganda, India, Pakistan, Australia and Spain, to name those which come quickly to mind. Single-deckers were supplied to virtually every country in the Commonwealth.

Then in the 1960s it all seemed to go wrong. Overseas became a place supplied by other manufacturers — giants like Mercedes or emerging manufacturers in the third world or Eastern Europe.

And so the great days of British exports overseas vanished — followed in short order by virtually all of Britain's automotive manufacturers. Cause and effect?

Why the duchess had to kick the bucket

Alan Millar

MY FAVOURITE STORY about London Transport has nothing to do with buses, tube trains or much else connected directly with transport. It's about fire buckets. But do read on. I promise you that there is a real bus connection.

Sometime around the late 1970s, one of many bunches of consultants unleashed on to LT visited the Acton Underground works. They were astounded to discover that when the hundreds of fire buckets scattered around the tube system corroded, Acton took them in, knocked out their rusty bottoms, welded on fine new bottoms, painted them in equally fine bright fire brigade red and sent them back out to the tube stations to keep potentially disastrous conflagrations at bay. Nothing wrong with that, except the consultants pointed out that this exercise was costing LT far more than it had sent someone round to Woolworth's in Acton High Street to buy new fire buckets. Like so much else it did, LT rewelded its fire buckets because it could do it, not because it had to.

It's a tiny symptom of what went wrong with LT at some time between the 1950s and 1970s, why this national institution which presumed to teach the rest of the world to run its buses and urban railways was itself in desperate need of outside advice. And why people like me — and many of you, I guess — also came to realise that the LT we had been brought up to revere was little more than a sham. An addled old duchess living on past glories and way beyond her means.

Open-mouthed wonderment

I don't know when all this dawned on me, whether it was before or after I made the 400-mile move from Glasgow to London in 1978, but the last vestiges of the illusion were hastened away after that move. Like many brought up in the days when enthusiast books and magazines were even less common than deregulated market town buses on a wet Sunday, I was exposed to a disproportionate amount of LT information in books, *Buses Illustrated* or publications like the *Meccano Magazine*. I still recall the open-mouthed wonderment with which I

Above: '... a late-1930s bus built to some of the highest design and manufacturing standards of the 1950s, a combination which guaranteed exceptionally long life for an essentially outdated design.' The classic London Routemaster, RM1871 temporarily renumbered SRM7 as one of the 25 RMs painted silver to mark the Queen's silver jubilee in 1977.
R. F. Mack

I greeted a *Look & Learn* feature on how Aldenham works could take RTs apart and reassemble them as new.

And it's not all illusion. There are things I will readily admit that LT has long done better than many other operators, like its comprehensive roadside timetable displays and the excellent standard of destination displays on most of its buses. Back in the late 1960s when Glasgow Corporation was trying to cram the origin and destination into what little remained of its front destination displays, its management came up with the preposterous assertion that LT's 'via' screens were unhelpful because you didn't know if the approaching bus had already passed Oxford Circus.

But I'm afraid these admirable practices don't excuse LT management its insularity of sheltering behind the Epstein statues at 55 Broadway and pretending that the outside world had nothing to teach it. For the shambles which manifested itself in the 1970s was born of such arrogance, a belief that LT was the biggest and best public transport organisation on the planet and that the words 'not invented here' were sufficient to dismiss most outside ideas.

What amazes me even now is that LT got away with it for so long. That it convinced not only itself, but the public, politicians and the national press that its misfortunes were visited upon it by some alien force and that none of the chickens coming home to roost had been hatched in its own coop.

Metropolitan mythology

I've been at dinner parties where ordinary, non-transport people have said that Metro-Cammell was the company that supplied London Transport with duff buses incapable of surviving one hour in London traffic. Yet by the time these seemingly informed people were relating such metropolitan mythology over their fondues, LT had wasted colossal sums of money specifying buses it then decided wouldn't work.

Between late-1969 and 1978 alone, LT bought 4,000 new buses — worth about £400 million at 1990s prices — which was enough to renew two-thirds of its fleet and give itself one of the most up-to-date bus operations in Europe. But when the last of these buses arrived, it was already planning their disposal; had used the newest ones to replace the first of the 4,000; was still running 30-year-old RTs and nearly-as-old RFs and was even looking on its next generation of buses as an expensive throw-away stop-gap.

With hindsight, I guess the rot had set in by the early 1950s when two seemingly forward-thinking decisions were taken. One was to develop the Routemaster, the other to build Aldenham works. To some *Classic Bus* readers, this may read like heresy, but I suggest both were steps too far and, like the fire buckets, they were done because LT could do it, not necessarily because it had to.

Now, don't get me wrong about the Routemaster. It's a fine bus, one of the most cleverly-designed buses ever conceived, a tremendously long-lasting one to boot and one whose sight still gladdens my eyes and ears on frequent visits to London or anywhere else they run, but I still question the wisdom of developing it.

The Routemaster was the logical progression beyond the highly-standardised RT family, of which 6,956 were built before production ended in 1954. The RT was a masterpiece well-suited to the needs of a huge undertaking which then ran over 8,000 buses in the most built-up part of Britain. Yet, for all its clever features, it wasn't vastly different from buses being bought by many other operators — something which helped relieve LT's embarrassment of finding it had bought more than it needed and had to start selling surplus postwar models as early as 1956.

But the Routemaster was different. Designed in the early 1950s to combine LT's bus operating and wartime aircraft manufacturing experience, its light, strong aluminium integral construction, hydraulic brakes and easily-removed major chassis units took the RT concept to such a point of perfection that over 600 were still running in London in 1994. But if it was so good, why did no other British city operator buy one? While their peers in Birmingham, Manchester, Leeds, Newcastle and Glasgow soon appreciated the

Top right: 'Hardly taxing work for the last bus designed totally for the needs of London.' The rear-engined Routemaster, FRM1, is seen on Round London Sightseeing Tour duties at Victoria in April 1982. Gavin Booth

Bottom right: 'If a bus reflected its owner, the DMS suggested LT was depressed, confused and out of control.' One of the earlier DMS-type Daimler Fleetlines with Park Royal bodywork, DMS203 of 1971, is still at work 10 years later. Gavin Booth

TOWN & COUNTRY
BUILDING SOCIETY
Lois
KGY 4D

Bloomsbury Waterloo
Elephant Bermondsey
Surrey Docks Deptford
188
EUSTON
Rothmans King Size
PLEASE PAY AS YOU ENTER
JGF203K

Left: The 50 Park Royal-bodied Leyland Atlanteans were based on a body style previously supplied to Stockton Corporation, and compared badly with LT's normal high standards of design. XA13 is pictured in Parliament Square on the 76 service. Gavin Booth

benefits of rear-engined Atlanteans and Fleetlines developed at the same time — and got to grips with their considerable teething problems — LT's bus managers went on buying about 300 open-platform Routemasters for each of the nine years until 1968 without gaining more than token experience of rear engines.

What they got was a late-1930s bus built to some of the highest design and manufacturing standards of the 1950s, a combination which guaranteed exceptionally long life for an essentially outdated design. More dangerously, they allowed its development to convince them that London needed a bus built exclusively for its special traffic conditions.

Masterpiece of the unnecessary

Aldenham fitted into this way of thinking. A vast green belt-factory designed to overhaul a standardised fleet somebody dreamt would one day reach 12,000; it was another masterpiece of the unnecessary. No other operator — not even the Tilling or BET groups — saw much need to separate chassis and body for major overhauls. And, as Mike Lloyd and David Thrower wrote in CB13, many outside LT regarded this factory — which once employed 1,800 people bussed in from all over Greater London — as an extremely expensive way of cleaning and repainting a bus.

By the time Aldenham was up and running in 1956 and Routemasters were entering service in 1959, LT was hitting deep trouble. Staff shortages, rising costs, increasing congestion and steadily falling patronage were plunging it into a financial crisis which high-tech old-fashioned buses and clever overhauling factories wouldn't solve.

Above: The rear-engined Routemaster, FRM1, which was banished to shuttle between West Croydon and Roundshaw, is seen in 1970. Edward Shirras

Above: MBA560, from the large batch of production AEC Merlins with Metro-Cammell bodies, is caught at Victoria on the 506 service in 1970. Alan Millar

It cruised the Caribbean and other waters in search of labour, but was fighting a losing battle and had to look rapidly for new operating methods like one-person operation.

So, in 1965 when big batches of Routemasters were still flowing in, it bought its first postwar rear-engined buses —15 Strachans-bodied AEC Merlin standee single-deckers and 50 Atlanteans and eight Fleetlines with Park Royal double-deck bodies. The Atlanteans were nominally red central area buses, the Fleetlines country buses, but some were swapped round to make comparisons between what were barely modified versions of the buses already running in some of the nation's biggest cities. Given their sheer lack of numbers, they passed through few LT employees' hands and, given LT's inexperience with rear engines and the indisputable problems with contemporary vehicles in other fleets, their trials were bound to be far from trouble-free.

Into this mix came a legend. FRM1, the solitary rear-engined Routemaster, was completed in 1966 and placed in service the following June. The project was already as good as dead, killed off by the Leyland Motor Corporation, government policy or LT's changing vehicle needs, depending on which demon you happen to favour least. But rather like John F. Kennedy after his assassination three years earlier, this prematurely slain bus acquired martyr status out of all proportion to its merits.

The FRM might well have developed into a fine bus, but it's also a fair bet that, had it lived to reach volume production, this Greatest Bus London Transport Never Had would have offered up its equivalent of the Vietnam War or Marilyn Monroe which tarnished Kennedy's later posthumous reputation. In their absence, its pedigree seemed perfect: 60% standard Routemaster body parts, Routemaster-derived rear axle, brakes, gearbox and engine. But the Atlantean had major units in common with the Titan PD3 and we all know they didn't always perform in perfect rear-engined harmony.

Nor does the FRM's track record seem entirely unblemished. It caught fire soon after entering service in central London and by late 1969 had begun its banishment to various outer reaches of the capital. It went first to Croydon where it shuttled to and from the Roundshaw housing estate, later to Potters Bar where LT's inflexibility dictated its only one-door opo 'decker had to go as route 284 was the only duty requiring a single bus. It ended up on the Round London Sightseeing

Tour which, while high profile, was hardly taxing work for the last bus designed totally for the needs of London.

If you don't accept the argument that Leyland killed the FRM out of some Atlantean-protecting spite, then the most likely cause was LT's Bus Reshaping Plan which was published three months before the FRM was first shown to the press. This was LT's radical — some might argue panic — plan for opo.

The Big One

Unlike the big city operators it no doubt scorned, LT had no reserves of rear-engined double-deckers which could be converted for conductor-less operation. So it went for the Big One: standee single-deckers on shortened suburban satellite routes feeding into hubs where passengers could change buses and maybe also use the Underground. Not only wasn't this going to need any sort of Routemaster, present or future, but it was to start being implemented within six months of the report being published and there was no time to develop a totally new bus. With only six of the 15 experimental Merlins running on the first Red Arrow route from Victoria to Marble Arch, LT committed itself to another 150 and before many of these were running placed a follow-up order for 450.

The Merlin was an AEC Swift with some relatively minor LT features added and fitted with the 11.3-litre AH691 engine found in few Swifts outside London. This was the horizontal version of the FRM's engine and, in light of early experience with the first Red Arrows, it was uprated from 147 to 165bhp for the 650 production buses. Park Royal still had nearly 200 Routemasters to complete, so Metro-Cammell Weymann — which had last supplied bus bodies to LT in the early 1950s — got the contract to build the lot to a variety of layouts, but to a design unique to LT.

On the standee buses, even the layouts were unique. Features like turnstiles and self-service ticket machines were scarcely seen north of Watford. Nor south of Walworth, for that matter, for they weren't found in many supposedly progressive European transport authorities' buses.

Yet LT, summoning up its best 'not invented here' voices, would soon be damning the Merlin as an off-the-peg design it had been compelled to buy. Certainly, it lacked the coil suspension, hydraulic brakes and integral construction of the Routemaster, but it was no more off-the-peg than the RT which had an LT-designed body on a modified provincial chassis. An ill-prepared urban operator's leap into large-scale rear-engined operation was surely far more of a problem, as was a reluctance to make them work.

Left: Some of the 164 London Scania-based MCW Metropolitans were withdrawn after only three years' service. MD66 was new in 1976, and may have been living on borrowed time when seen in 1981 passing the Imperial War Museum. Gavin Booth

Nor did LT seem to realise how big these buses were. Neither its garages nor some tight corners in the suburbs could accommodate 11metre buses too easily. The Metropolitan Police compounded the difficulty by preventing Merlins from running anywhere they might have to cross a white line to turn left.

Subsequent orders had to be for 10m buses and that meant a big power sacrifice. The short Swift could only accommodate the 8.2-litre AH505 engine — the Routemaster, RT and RF had 9.6-litre engines — but LT ordered 838 for delivery between late-1969 and early-1972, its last-ever AECs. MCW, Park Royal and Marshall fitted them with a scaled down Merlin body, the chassis still had some unique LT features and they were all, of course, considered to be underpowered off-the-peg atrocities.

By then, LT had waded far deeper and longer than any British big city operator in the muddy waters of first generation standee single-deck operation. Only Liverpool and Leeds showed anything like this commitment and they returned to double-deckers far sooner. When LT came under Greater London Council control in January

Above: The London Bristol LHs 'led short and unhappy lives'. BL15, an LH6L model with ECW 39-seat body, is seen in Romford when new in 1976. Gavin Booth

1970, 109 country department Merlins stayed in state ownership with the National Bus Company's new London Country company which also got 138 of the Swifts when they were built.

The DMS is born

That left LT with 1,256 Merlins and Swifts, or about a fifth of its total fleet. It was at saturation level and returned to double-deckers from 1970. The earlier trials favoured the Fleetline over the Atlantean (all 50 of which soon were shipped to Hong Kong) and thus was born the DMS and its derivatives of which 2,646 were bought over the next eight years, roughly two-thirds with Park Royal bodies, the rest from MCW.

Chassis modifications included automatic transmission and AEC-type steering wheels, while the manufacturers' already very similar standard bodies were substantially redesigned to incorporate LT requirements which included a bottom deck which was a shortened and rearranged version of the standee single-deckers, complete with turnstiles and self-service ticket machines seldom used by passengers.

The resultant bus, to put it kindly, looked disappointing. None of the careful design of the Routemaster or even the relative brightness of the Merlins and Swifts survived into what LT briefly and unsuccessfully tried to brand the Londoner. The name reflected the inspiration of LT's new bus boss — later its chairman — Ralph Bennett who, as general manager in Manchester, had introduced the far more exciting Mancunian two years earlier. If a bus reflected its owner, the DMS suggested LT was depressed, confused and out of control.

Most DMSs and the crew-operated versions — bought after the GLC froze extensions of opo in the mid-1970s — had either Gardner 6LXB or Leyland 680 engines, but there were a few with Rolls-Royce engines. And the last 400 came to LT's unique B20 specification with lightly turbocharged Leyland 690 engine and asymmetric chimneys at the back which were supposed to make them quieter but not such as you would notice. They whined like gigantic industrial vacuum cleaners.

In 1976/77, they were accompanied by 164 crew-operated Metropolitans with Scania running units and MCW bodies which went into a couple of southeast London garages. They reintroduced dual sourcing of LT buses for the first time since the last RTLs were bought in 1954 and, although modified for LT, were much closer to the manufacturer's standard specification than any of the DMSs.

But the 1970s were when LT's bus buying went mad. The Routemaster had been designed to last 17 years and in the normal course of events and with bus grants keeping up the level of fleet replacements, it was anticipated that the last RTs and RFs would go around 1974, the Routemasters would go next and the Merlins would go by 1980/81. But the Merlin 'wasn't invented here', had suffered its share of chassis and body problems and there was still the monster of Aldenham to consider.

A pilot overhaul of a Strachans-bodied Merlin

Above: The interiors of the Red Arrow Merlins were designed for maximum passenger flow, but were hardly the most inviting vehicles. A 6d piece in the slot machine on the right released the turnstile and if passengers were lucky they might be among the 25 sittees.

took most of 1972, convinced the self-styled best bus operator in the world that the task was prohibitive for a plant geared up to large numbers of double-deckers and withdrawal began almost by stealth. In August 1973, LT persuaded the GLC to bring forward their replacement by five years. Within a year, hundreds were being stored in corners of bus and rail depots as LT tried to sell them far enough away from Britain for its sales spiel to get to potential buyers before they heard its home market excuses for their disposal. The truth must have travelled fast for, by July 1975, Merlins were piling up so rapidly that open-air secure space was rented in Radlett airfield in Hertfordshire and 300 were stored there by the end of the year. Many were still there two years later when the site was vacated; the asking price reputedly was cut from £9,000 to £2,000 and most went for scrap.

About the biggest buyer for further service was Citybus which needed replacements for buses destroyed in riots and terrorist attacks in Belfast. At an industry function soon after buying them, Ulsterbus / Citybus's redoubtable then-managing director, Werner Heubeck, suggested mischievously that LT should sack the man who sold them to him — because they were so good.

Maybe LT was beginning to think so, too, for it hung on to about 70 until 1981 for the Red Arrow network, a heavily peaked operation in the densest London traffic conditions. So much for off-the-peg buses failing to cut the London mustard. But most others were withdrawn by the end of 1976. By then, the GLC had approved the replacement of the 700 Swifts and the last RTs and RFs, mainly with DMSs and Metropolitans, but also with an eventual fleet of 437 Mk1 and 69 Mk2 Leyland Nationals — totally off-the-peg buses designed with more than half an eye on the London market.

Some RF routes were deemed unsuitable for bigger buses and after a trawl of the limited selection of small vehicles then on the market, LT plumped for 95 mildly modified ECW-bodied Bristol LHs which were scattered in small batches around mainly outer-suburban garages. That didn't help anyone get on top of the LHs and these, too, led short and unhappy lives. In Sutton, where I lived in the early 1980s, an LH route was suddenly found to be capable of accommodating DMSs.

These experiences were reinforcing LT's conviction that only it knew how to design buses for London and its engineers were working on a project code-named XRM by the early 1970s. No prizes for guessing its ancestry.

Never taken beyond the drawing board and model stage, this was what the Routemaster perhaps ought to have been 20 years earlier. It was to have a side engine, so could either be a

Below: One of the shorter SMS-type Swifts is pictured at Southgate in 1973 alongside one of LT's first 20 minibuses, 1972 Ford Transits, with 16-seat Strachan bodywork. Alan Millar

Above: The first of the DMS-type Daimler Fleetlines, DMS1, is seen at the Park Royal coachworks prior to its appearance at the 1970 Commercial Show. The fairly stark lines of the body are evident, not helped by the all-over red livery. Park Royal

two-door opo bus or an open-platform Routemaster replacement. With less engine intrusion, it could be shorter and more manoeuvrable in traffic and in LT's garages. Many of its benefits could be bought off-the-peg with the front-engined Ailsa launched in 1973, but LT showed no interest in it until it was going out of production in 1983.

Instead, it let Aldenham determine the DMS's fate. Still wishing it could separate bodies and chassis unlike any other operator in the country, it despaired of being able to overhaul the Fleetlines and got GLC approval to sell them too. Claims of their unsuitability for London traffic seemed odd when few penetrated the heart of London. Were the conditions in central Croydon, Hounslow or Romford any worse than central Birmingham or Manchester where Fleetlines ran without threats of their imminent demise?

Bargain prices

The argument seemed even less sustainable when West Midlands and Greater Manchester PTEs were among the operators — many of them starved of Fleetlines in the mid-1970s when LT deliveries took priority — which snapped up bargain-priced DMSs on the second-hand market. So did numerous NBC, municipal, Scottish Bus Group and independent operators. They went in big numbers to Hong Kong where traffic and atmospheric conditions aren't known to be gentle and later — surely to LT's embarrassment — they were used to compete against their former owner on sightseeing tours and tendered bus routes. With them went the Metropolitans, some withdrawn after three years' service, but victims of design faults experienced by most of their other customers, so let's not blame LT for that one.

All were replaced by 1,440 Mk1 MCW Metrobuses and 1,125 Leyland Titans bought between 1978 and 1985. Both were off-the-peg designs based on the lessons learned in London and other cities and the Titan, which sold hardly anywhere else and bristled with features inspired by the legendary FRM, was kept in production at LT's insistence when Leyland would gladly have supplied modified Olympians at less cost.

But even these were viewed with less than total favour by some at LT. In a last blast of atavism, it went on a Routemaster buying spree. It snapped up most of London Country's coaches and buses when they were withdrawn in the late 1970s and put most in passenger, staff bus or driving school service. It bought British Airways' forward-entrance coaches for a variety of limited uses like bussing workers to Aldenham and even bought 12 forward-entrance buses withdrawn by Northern General — the only Routemaster customer outside London — but gave them up as a bad job.

And it let it be known that it only saw the Titan and Metrobus as a stopgap until the XRM was ready for a manufacturer to build from the mid-1980s. Crazier still, far from planning to replace any of its beloved Routemasters, it was talking of starting with opo XRMs to clear out the Titans and Metrobuses by the early 1990s before taking open platform XRMs into the fleet and finally pensioning off the Routemasters.

Fortunately, sense prevailed. A different sort of stopgap, Sir Peter Masefield — the chairman appointed hurriedly when Ralph Bennett was pushed out by the GLC in 1980 and who ended up staying nearly two years till a more permanent successor was found — axed a bus unlikely to have sold elsewhere and LT began learning to live with buses which were much better than their immediate predecessors.

The duchess's corpse did twitch a bit longer. The Labour GLC elected in 1981 talked of revitalising the London bus manufacturing industry by sponsoring a factory to build Routemasters which, in turn, would employ more conductors. It only

talked about it. LT later commissioned Ogle Design to develop a bus with features geared to London operation. Ogle's thoughts included features long-tried in other British cities and also a curious idea of a cutaway front nearside platform — a sort of Routemaster in reverse. A few bits made their way into production, but just a few.

LT, freed from some of its most stifling bureaucracy, was plunging fast into reality. It was trying first small batches, later big ones, of true off-the-peg buses. It kept and re-engined most of the B20 Fleetlines, rescued some earlier ones from its sales department and in one of the biggest known swallowings of corporate pride bought 14 DMSs back from Clydeside Scottish as dozens of surplus Routemasters went in the opposite direction. And Aldenham, whose high costs must at least have matched the extra costs of running the much derided off-the-peg Merlins, Swifts and Fleetlines, was finally closed in 1986.

But what a long time it took. What a waste of resources. Of money. Of people's efforts. And to what benefit for LT's long-suffering and diminishing numbers of passengers? Hardly the actions of an organisation which prided itself in still being a world leader. And to think those consultants only got as far as the fire buckets.

Top: It would appear that the B20 Fleetlines with the lightly turbocharged Leyland 690 engine were no more reliable than their normally-aspirated brothers. This is a 1983 scene. Gavin Booth

Above: LT's 1970s 'Routemaster buying spree' included RCL-type coaches bought from London Country. Some were put into service as red buses, retaining their original style of blind display and rear platform, though without the doors. RCL2222 is seen at Victoria in March 1983, during its three-year stint as a bus. Gavin Booth

---

Alan Millar is a freelance transport journalist who writes for a broad range of publications and has written a number of bus books.

Left: The first Daimler Fleetline, DMS1, viewed from the rear.
Park Royal

Left: An all-too familiar rear view of a DMS — broken down at the roadside with its engine cover open.
Stewart J. Brown

Left: A British Leyland official view shows two early DMSs. The original BL caption suggests that they were Leyland 680-engined, but this variation did not come along until 1972.

Top: All stockpiled and nowhere to go. Some of the hundreds of Merlins stored at Radlett aerodrome between 1975 and 1977. Not only did LT reputedly have to knock £7,000 off the book value of each bus, but it also incurred substantial, but never disclosed, storage costs while 70 similar buses remained at work on Red Arrow routes in the heart of the City and the West End. Capital Transport

Above: Yet another new type launched for London Transport — the first three Leyland Titans do a circuit of Parliament Square for the cameras in 1978. Leyland

SOUTH WALES SELECTION

P. R. WALLIS photographs of South Wales Transport buses in the 1960s.

South Wales Transport was set up in 1914 by the British Electric Traction Co to operate connecting bus services from its Swansea trams, but by 1937 SWT buses had replaced the Swansea trams and the company had grown by natural expansion and takeover. Postwar acquisitions included the Llanelly trolleybus system — bought and closed down in 1952 — and fellow BET operator, James of Ammanford. SWT was a committed AEC user, and the James takeover brought Leylands into the fleet. Today, SWT survives as a company in the Badgerline group.

Philip Wallis lived in Baughurst, Hampshire, close to a small Venture depot, where friendly staff helped him to become a bus enthusiast at the age of four. Following schooldays he undertook engineering training at Thornycroft in Basingstoke, followed by a period of commissioned service in the Royal Engineers. Since that time he has worked in sales and executive capacities in the construction plant and agricultural machinery industries. He has always maintained a strong interest in the bus industry and is a keen bus photographer.

Above: Photographed at Ammanford in August 1961, a 1947 James Leyland Tiger PS1 that had lost its Strachan bus body in 1955 in favour of this Weymann Orion 55-seat lowbridge body. All photographs by P. R. Wallis

Above: Looking slightly odd in South Wales red, No 1111, a 1953 all-Leyland PD2/12 lowbridge, was one of two acquired with the James business. It is seen in July 1963 at Ammanford.

Below: Still in James colours, but wearing SWT fleetnumber 804, this was one of six Weymann-bodied Leyland Tiger Cub PSUC1/1 that passed to South Wales. These buses would really have been more at home in the fleet of neighbouring BET company, Western Welsh.

Above: James was an early customer for the Leyland Atlantean — indeed its first was one of the four prototypes exhibited at the 1958 Commercial Motor Show — and this is its second, new in 1959 with Metro-Cammell 73-seat semi-lowbridge bodywork.

Below: Leaving the Ammanford depot/bus station bound for Swansea in July 1963, No 950 was one of three Leyland Leopard PSU3/3s ordered by James but delivered to South Wales after the takeover in 1963. They had Marshall 53-seat bodywork.

Above: This James Leyland Titan PD2/12 with Metro-Cammell 59-seat lowbridge body was new in 1957 and passed to South Wales as its No 1222 in 1962, a year after this photograph was taken at Ammanford.

Below: Weymann-bodied AEC Regents, in both highbridge and lowbridge form, were standard South Wales double-deck purchases for many years. This 1949 Regent III, with 56-seat highbridge body, is seen in Swansea in 1961.

Above: Ten of the 1957 Regent Vs had Willowbrook 60-seat highbridge bodies, like No 498 seen in Swansea in 1961.

Below: South Wales was a big user of forward-entrance 30ft Regent Vs. This Weymann-bodied 71-seat example was one of 33 bought in 1958/9, and is seen in Swansea in 1961.

Left: No 424 was one of a batch of 11 AEC Regent IIIs with Weymann bodies ordered by Llanelly District Traction, but delivered direct in 1952 to South Wales, where they appeared to be very much at home. It is seen in Llanelly in 1963.

Left: AEC Regent IIIs with the Birmingham style of tin front were only found in a small number of fleets. South Wales took a batch with Weymann 53-seat lowbridge bodies in 1954, before AEC developed the Regent V with its distinctive front-end. No 1185 is seen in Llanelly in 1963.

Left: Low-height single-deckers were necessary for routes in the Llanelly Docks area, and in 1959/62 South Wales bought eight of these AEC Regent V with 8ft 11in high Roe 37-seat bodies. No 35, of the 1962 batch, is seen in Llanelly the following year.

Left: The first AEC Regent V for South Wales were 1955 examples with Weymann bodies, some highbridge and some lowbridge. No 446, a highbridge example, is seen in Llanelly in 1963.

Left: Two Weymann-bodied AEC Regents in Llanelly in 1963: Regent V No 503 of 1958 is followed by a 1952 Regent III.

Left: The first South Wales 36ft AEC Reliance, No 953 with Marshall 53-seat body, in Llanelly in 1963.

Above: Another bus from the 1958 batch, one of 13 supplied in unpainted aluminium finish, a fashion of the late 1950s.

.Above: South Wales also bought forward-entrance Regent Vs with Willowbrook bodies, like No 543 of 1960 photographed in Swansea the following year.

Right: For its low-height needs, South Wales moved on to the AEC Bridgemaster and then the Renown. Bridgemaster No 1216, new in 1961, is seen that year in Swansea. The 72-seat bodywork was by Park Royal.

Right: This style of Park Royal body found its way into the Top Ten Ugliest Buses, voted by readers of *Classic Bus.* Fitted here to AEC Bridgemaster No 1217, the rear view is not one of its strong points, hardly helped by the all-red South Wales 'livery'.

Above: Fishwick's No 17, a 1929 Leyland Tiger TS1, seen in the garage yard at Golden Hill, Leyland, is a good example of the company's purchases of all-Leyland single-deckers in the prewar years.
Ribble Enthusiasts Club

SURPRISES JUST AROUND THE CORNER

PETER HESKETH recalls some of the more unusual vehicles that have operated for Fishwick of Leyland

RODGERS AND HAMMERSTEIN, Marx and Engels, London Transport and the Associated Equipment Co; over the years, some names have become inextricably linked. With Leyland Motors no more than a cock-stride away from its Golden Hill headquarters it was always inevitable that John Fishwick & Sons would form a strong association with it. From the inception of operations to Preston, Chorley and other destinations in 1910, Leyland Motors products were the natural preference. Those familiar with this central Lancashire independent are no doubt well aware that unusual vehicles have featured in the fleet from time to time, but a closer look reveals less obvious facts surrounding the Fishwick purchasing policy.

Choice of bodywork in earlier days was notable as Leyland's own did not always figure. Up to and including the receipt of its TD1 Titans, Leyland bodies had been specified for both single-deck and double-deck vehicles, However, during the remainder of the prewar era it was only single-deckers that were to carry this make, Burlingham bodywork being applied to double-deckers. All chassis were, of course, Leylands. The first from Burlingham, mounted on TD4 chassis in 1935 and were unusual in themselves by being rather antiquated-looking at a time when Leyland was busy marketing its vee-front all-metal design. In effect they were identical to the original 'piano-front' style, and as Northern Counties and Massey Brothers built similar for Wigan Corporation at this time it is not unreasonable to speculate as to whether Leyland disposed of its surplus and now-redundant body frames for that type, to those three builders. One of these, ironically, did end up with a Leyland vee-front body, but only after sale to nearby Bamber Bridge Motor Services, when in 1953 it received the one from BBMS's own No 4, a TD3 it had bought new, the chassis being then scrapped. (This is only part of BBMS's rebodying

Left: An early postwar view of Fishwick's 1935 Leyland Titan TD4, No 4, fitted with a Burlingham body of rather antiquated styling, very similar to Leyland's 'piano-front' design, which gives rise to a theory put forward in the text. Leyland

Left: Fishwick's Leyland/Burlingham association was reversed after the war, with Leyland supplying complete double-deckers, such as No 32, a Titan PD1 seen leaving Ribble's old Preston bus station in Tithebarn Street on a works service to its birthplace. R. H. G. Simpson

Left: It was almost inevitable that Fishwick would choose the locally-built all-Leyland product, like this 1948 Titan PD2.
Dale Tringham Collection

Top left: Burlingham bodywork was to be found on early postwar Fishwick saloons. No 34 was a Tiger PS1 dating from 1949, photographed at Golden Hill on 11 April 1954.
Roy Marshall

Middle left: Eight integral Leyland/MCW Olympic HR44 were bought by Fishwick in 1951. No 16 is seen leaving Preston and crossing the railway station bridge *en route* for Chorley when new.
R. H. G. Simpson

Bottom left: Fishwick No 11, a Leyland Leopard PSU3/3R, was fitted with 45-seat Weymann bodywork to the early style that predated the more familiar BET design. It is seen in 1966.
Roger Holmes

tale, intriguing in its own right, but not to be enlarged upon here!) Four new TD5s appeared in 1937, again fitted with lowbridge Burlingham bodies, but this time to the current Ribble specification.

Concurrent with this, all-Leyland TS8 Tigers employing metal frames were bought. Could it have been that Fishwick was not prepared to put all its eggs in the Leyland bodyshop basket too soon? It was obviously aware of Leyland's none-too-successful early attempts at all-metal construction and perhaps preferred to stick to Burlingham's timber-framed 'deckers, whilst

testing that water with just a few saloons. However, after inactivity in the vehicle front during the war, when no utilities were added, the Leyland / Burlingham situation was reversed. The first new vehicles in the postwar period were PD1 Titans, and now it was Leyland who provided complete double-deckers, whereas Burlingham built single-deck saloon bodies (still timber-framed) on PS1 Tigers. These were to be Burlingham's last contributions, even though it

Above left: Fishwick had its own bus station in Fox Street, Preston, before the new station was opened in 1969, although some services had carried on up to Ribble's in Tithebarn Street. Fox Street is the location for this view of all-Leyland Titan PD2/12 No 6, shortly after delivery in 1954. Note the smaller metal, rubber-glazed upper-deck emergency exit which featured on small numbers of Leyland bodies just prior to the cessation of bodybuilding. This bus was later fitted with platform doors. Peter Hesketh Collection

Below left: A pair of angular-looking Leyland Tiger Cubs with Massey bodies appeared in 1966 and were to have an influence on the company's bodywork policy in the years to follow. Chorley bus station is the location of No 2 seen here. R. H. G. Simpson

Above: An ex-demonstrator taken into stock in 1969 was No 1, the Park Royal-bodied Leyland Panther PSUR1/1R, JTJ 667F, which had its centre door removed prior to entering service. No other Panthers were bought. Peter Hesketh

Right: Only one double-deck body was attempted by Fishwick's associated company, Fowlers, with none-too-pleasing results. No 6 was based on an Atlantean PDR1/3 chassis bought by Fishwick in 1970 and stored until 1973. If the need had arisen, it could have been converted to dual-door layout and, as can be seen, bulkheads were in position and an inward-facing seat was fitted in the space behind the front axle where the exit would have gone. Ribble Enthusiasts Club

was to be more than ten years before the company ceased production.

Last Faringtons

Batches of all-Leyland double-deckers were bought right up to the end of body production at the Farington plant, and the last came into the fleet in 1954 were interesting in one small respect. In the last couple of years some highbridge bodies by Leyland featured a shallower variant of the two-piece rear upper-deck emergency exit, which was also different from the previous standard in that it was made of metal, and rubber-glazed. Apart from Fishwick and Leyland itself, for a demonstrator (STC 887, later Scout's No 20), it is probable that only Midland Red, Trent and Manchester Corporation specified this type of exit. Postwar vehicle input had nevertheless been far from standard insofar as saloons were concerned, as no fewer than eight of Leyland's revolutionary

Above: Seen at Golden Hill in June 1975, are Leyland Atlantean AN68/1R No 18, with East Lancs 74-seat body, one of two, and Daimler Fleetline SRL6/36 No 20, with 48-seat body, one of three locally built by Fishwick associate, Fowler. Both buses were new in 1974. Roger Holmes

Above: Fishwick was a natural home for Leyland demonstrators. This prototype Titan was one of two acquired in the early 1980s, this one after a period of extended loan. FHG 592S was Titan prototype B15.02, built in 1974 but not registered until 1977, and is seen in 1984 after crossing the West Coast Main Line at Leyland. Gavin Booth

Above: One of the East Lancs-bodied Atlanteans is seen flanked by Fishwick's two former experimental AN69 Atlanteans. No 23 (left), with ECW body of a style fitted to many Atlanteans, was used as a testbed for the London Transport B20 'quiet' Fleetline; No 2 (right) was originally left-hand drive, and carries Olympian-style ECW bodywork. Peter Hesketh

underfloor-engined integral Olympics, produced in collaboration with Metropolitan-Cammell Weymann, were bought. Classified as HR44, Fishwick's came, as all home models did after the initial MCW prototypes, from the Weymann factory. The marque did not find universal favour on the home market when compared with its chassised Royal Tiger counterpart but this did not deter Leyland and MCW launching a lightweight version based on Tiger Cub components in 1953, closely named the Olympian. Like the Olympic this new chassisless model also failed to live up to expectations as far as sales were concerned.

Fishwick had the only Lancashire examples, six being purchased in 1957, a year before the Olympian was deleted from the catalogue. These deliveries left MCW's mark on the company, and it was this company which supplied all bodywork until 1966 on PD2/40 Titan, Leopard and Atlantean chassis.

In 1963, Fishwick acquired the coaching business of J. & R. Singleton, also of Leyland. (Fishwick and Ribble had jointly purchased the stage carriage side of the firm in 1935.) Thus Fishwick, after over 50 years' existence, finally entered the excursion trade and began replacing the Singleton fleet, which turned up some unusual vehicles in the process. Amongst those bought new initially, were a pair of Albion Victor VT21Ls with Duple Firefly bodies, which introduced a lilac and purple coach livery, a contrast to the standard (then and now) two-tone green. At the same time a separate numbering series with C prefixes was applied to the coach fleet. Such was the success of the Singleton acquisition that business rapidly expanded and by way of a stopgap until new coaches were received, a couple of the Olympians were refurbished by Duple (Northern). Coach seats were fitted, along with new floors, luggage lockers, radios and side mouldings. Coach livery was carried. Once pressure eased they were painted back into bus green, but retained the mouldings as shade dividers which gave them a distinctive appearance.

Surprisingly, ex-Leyland demonstrators have never featured in large numbers until comparatively recently. In fact only two pure sales demonstrators have been owned. The first, SGD 669, was a PDR1/1 Atlantean, originally supplied to Glasgow Corporation in 1963 but bought back by Leyland the following year and then sold to Fishwick in 1965. Alexander bodywork was carried, the only example of this make ever in stock. Another unique chassis type for the company was its second, JTJ 667F, a Park Royal-bodied PSUR1/1R dual-door Panther, put into service in 1969 after its centre door had been blanked off. Furthermore the company has never been a large purchaser of other second-hand buses either, although in more recent times used coaches have featured. The first was a 1963 Duple (Northern)-bodied Leopard, which came from Leyland Motors Sports and Social Club in 1966. Over 20 years later, the aftermath of deregulation in 1986 has seen low-mileage used coaches being snapped up. Apart from this modern coaching trend, the only second-hand saloons acquired were four Leyland Nationals; three came from Lancaster in 1978 and one from Rennie of Dunfermline. The latter concern sold its 'one-off' 10.9m DP45F model in 1981 and Fishwick increased its capacity to 49 with bus seats. At the same time one of the Fowler-bodied Leopards (described next) was sold to Rennie. (As, indeed, were many Fishwick vehicles over the years.)

Lancashire bodies

As I have stated, the MCW influence did not fade until the mid-1960s. After the Burlingham PS1s no Lancashire body manufacturer managed to get a foot into the Golden Hill garage door until Massey Brothers bodied a pair of angular-looking Tiger Cubs. This style perhaps had an influence on what happened next. Fowlers, a local associated company of Fishwick, acquired in 1966, who amongst other things, adapted lorry cabs to provide sleeping accommodation, turned its hand to bus bodybuilding up to the end of the decade and into the early 1970s. All told, it built 12, all except one (a coach-bodied Seddon for Duckworth's of Gisburn, near Clitheroe) for Fishwick. The first constructed was a 12-seater based on a Ford Transit in 1968, followed by a 44-seat saloon on the very last Tiger Cub chassis in 1969. Then came three Leopards, all of which, although angular and having more than just a passing resemblance to the Massey bodies mentioned, were not unattractive. This could not be said of Fowler's only attempt at a double-deck body, mounted on a PDR1/3 Atlantean chassis in 1973, which had, in fact, been owned and stored for three years. There was no noticeable inward cant to the upper deck, which gave it a blatantly top-heavy look. It had been built in such a way as to enable a centre exit to be fitted should the then Central Lancashire New Town expand to the degree that was then hoped. Thankfully the town did not, and much beautiful, unspoilt countryside around Preston and Leyland remained that way — and again, perhaps thankfully, the Atlantean's life-span was not particularly long.

Fowler's final fling came in 1973 when it all but doubled its production thus far — on what was for Fishwick, on the face of it — an unusual chassis order, to say the least. In that year Daimler Fleetline assembly was transferred by its parent company, British Leyland, from Coventry to Leyland, and five SRL6/36 models were acquired. Like the Cub and Leopards they were quite well-proportioned, with their 48-seat bodies having an extra capacity for 20 standees. They incorporated KL Automative forced ventilation (standard on all Fowler bodies) and the first two had stepped seating. This was to accommodate an intended centre exit, but it was decided not to include this feature and the later trio had a straight upward-sloping floor. The aforementioned Panther adaptation was in line with this thinking.

Inevitably, pure Leylands were soon back in favour in the form of AN68 Atlanteans, and, what is more, another local body supplier, East Lancashire, made its mark by bodying all this chassis type for Fishwick between 1973 and 1977.

Although only two demonstrators have been owned, prototype and experimental vehicles have been more numerous.

Above: Carrying an unusual variation to the Fishwick livery, No 25, one of the Titan TN prototypes (B15.04) with Park Royal bodywork, leaves Tuer Street, Golden Hill, *en route* to Preston on 30 April 1983. By this time it was in Fishwick ownership and had lost its centre exit. Roy Marshall

Left: Fowler's final fling came in 1973 when five Daimler Fleetline SRL/36 chassis, built at Leyland Motors, were fitted with 48-seat bodies. No 9 was one of the last three, with a sloping floor. Peter Hesketh

Of the five prototype new generation TN series Titans built by Leyland between 1975 and 1977, three ended up in Fishwick ownership, after intermittent periods on loan to the company, to build up in-service mileage. During the loan period, a variety of liveries could be seen on them, including Fishwick's own, and London Transport red.

The current double-deck fleet is smaller than it was in the 1950s, single-deckers now maintaining stage carriage services. However, the five surviving 'deckers, used mainly for contract work, have two veritable gems amongst their numbers and are a present day epitome of the raison d'être of this article. Both are Atlanteans and both are the later post-PDR AN type, but there the normality ends. Whilst AN68s were produced in quantity, only two AN69 chassis ever saw the light of day, and these are the pair with Fishwick. In 1981 the first, with a then standard ECW normal-height body, appeared. Its chassis, though, dated from 1975 and had been used as a test-bed for the London Transport B20 'quiet' Fleetline, its rear-end bustle with its large air intakes giving the game away. Its stablemate arrived three years later in 1984, this time on a longer AN69/2L chassis, originally with left-hand drive. Once converted, it received an Olympian-style ECW body, identical to Preston's example, which was used by Leyland as a demonstrator, and having two small windows amidships on each deck to give it the extra length required.

Leyland vehicles are now losing their strength within the Fishwick fleet. The arrival of minibuses of Mercedes-Benz manufacture and the purchase of Bovas, Volvos and DAFs on the coach side (which, incidentally, is now back in green livery, with areas of white) plus Leyland's cessation of Lynx production, have heralded a new look on the horizon.

This has not been intended as a definitive study of Fishwick's vehicles but rather a look at the unusual amongst them. We can rest assured that individuality and the occasional surprise will now and again creep into Golden Hill Lane from the Fishwick premises, although initial journeys for these future buses and coaches will, sadly, not be passing the imposing gates of their birthplace, Leyland Motors, just around the corner.

Durham's trolleybuses

PETER DURHAM studies of preserved trolleybuses

Right: Maidstone Corporation operated trolleybuses from 1928 until 1967, and No 56 was one of three 1944 Sunbeam Ws which had their utility Park Royal bodies replaced by new Roe 62-seat bodies in 1960. All photographs by Peter Durham

Right: Wolverhampton No 433 was another 1945 Sunbeam W with utility Park Royal bodywork that received a new Roe body, this time in 1959. It was one of 15 similar vehicles in the sizeable Wolverhampton trolleybus fleet. Wolverhampton operated trolleybuses from 1923 until 1967.

Photos taken at the Black Country Museum, near Dudley.

Left:
This impressive beast was one of 12 Sunbeam S7s with Park Royal 68-seat bodies bought by Reading Corporation in 1950 to cope with increased passenger loadings on the 'mainline' trolleybus routes. Now owned by M. J. Russell, No 174 was exhibited at the 1950 Commercial Motor Show. It was withdrawn in November 1968 after taking part in the procession to mark the end of 32 years of trolleybus operation in the town.

Left:
The last batch of new trolleybuses bought for service in Britain were nine Sunbeam MF2B with Weymann 65-seat two-door bodies for Bournemouth Corporation. There should have been 10 of these attractive vehicles, but one chassis was destroyed in a fire at Weymanns. New in 1962, they were withdrawn after only seven years service, when the Bournemouth system closed.

Left:
One of the last British trolleybus systems to close was Teesside Municipal Transport. Trolleybuses operated on Teesside from 1919 until 1971, and No T291 was one of five attractive 1961 Sunbeam F4As with Burlingham 68-seat bodies acquired in 1969, after the Reading system closed.

SUSSEX SUNDAE

MICHAEL DRYHURST serves up a confection of memories in forties and fifties flashback

IT WAS so normal, it was never thought worth commenting upon, the fact that virtually each and every bus company, its operations and its vehicles, would be different and distinctive, individual and almost indigenous to each respective operator. No two companies were alike, and even my memory of the supposedly highly-standardised Tilling group with its conformity to the products of Bristol and Eastern Coach Works recalls very individual fleets — Bristol with its PD1 Leyland Titans, many locally-bodied, and Bedford OBs; Crosville with both AEC and Leyland postwar deliveries plus Bedfords; Cumberland with its large Leyland fleet bodied by many companies other than ECW; Hants & Dorset with its PD-Titans and Regent lll AECs' plus the great mix of coach bodies on its Bristol L-series… and so on. And then of course, there was the Brighton, Hove & District Omnibus Co with its non-standard destination screens and very much the Tilling group exception in not operating a single lowbridge double-decker!

'Brighton, Hove & District Transport' was the working title of the Brighton Corporation Transport Department and the BH&DOC, which operating merger came about as a result of the 1938 Brighton Corporation Act whereby the two concerns entered into an operating agreement, including a livery and destination layout common to the vehicles of both.

The Sussex branch of Thomas Tilling Ltd, which was eventually to become BH&D, operated a large fleet of AEC Regent I 661 buses of the company's standard, known generically as the 'Tilling ST', and my earliest recollection of the Hove company's vehicles were of these buses, although many had been rebuilt even to the extent of enclosing the rear staircase, and considerable numbers were rebodied. But by 1946 the BH&D Tilling STs were a very sorry sight and I associate them most with route 6, Fishersgate-Brighton station, which passed my prep school and proved to be of greater (and more enduring…) interest than either mensa, a table, or the Hundred Years War. On some, the lower-deck waistrail sagged so much as to appear like an inverted bow! First-hand riding of these AECs was common in that the school on New Church Road did not boast any games pitches, so on Tuesday and Thursday afternoons in the winter and spring terms we were

pposite top: **Brighton Hove & District was allocated ? utility buses — two Mk1 Guy Arabs and two atches of Bristol K6A, the only examples of this odel delivered new to the company; the 10 AEC-ngined buses carried Park Royal bodies. This is No 366 of the first batch, seen after the rebuilding by H&D which resulted in a larger windscreen. The enue is Church Road, Hove, with 1949 K5G, No 409, following and, in the distance, the tower of ove Town Hall, long since destroyed by fire.** Aichael Dryhurst

pposite below: **Among the earliest postwar single-eck deliveries to Southdown was a number of eyland Tiger PS1 fitted with Eastern Coach Works 31-seat rear-entrance bodywork to coach specification, painted in an attractive two-tone green, and cream, livery. This shows No 1244 in as-delivered state with its ECW standard sliding ventilators, replaced shortly thereafter by Southdown with half-drops.**

bussed to Hove Park for our rugger games, and these venerable AECs were the usual choice of BH&D for such a day.

The deliveries to the company in the mid-1930s were quite varied. The first locally-registered AEC Regents (the Tilling STs had all carried London County Council registrations) were followed by a small batch of Dennis Ace saloons for one-man operation on lightly-trafficked routes and then some Dennis Lance I double-deckers with Tilling-style bodies, these being followed by the first Bristols, GO5G chassis with Eastern Counties bodies, a final brace of AEC Regents and then more Bristols. One final Ace was received late in the decade proving to be the last purchase of saloons by BH&D for some 20 years; from 1946 -1959 the BH&D fleet was all double-deck. Earlier Dennis single-deckers had been some Darts, purchased during the Tilling era.

Doubly unusual

Bristol K5G buses followed on from the GO5Gs, 18 such vehicles being delivered up to 1940. During the war came a couple of MkI Guy Arabs, doubly unusual in carrying austerity bodywork by Pickering, and then 10 K6A Bristols that carried Park Royal utility bodywork. The initial postwar Bristol delivery were Nos 6376-85, of which the first eight were model K5G, the remainder model K6B, all 10 buses carrying the well-proportioned no-nonsense ECW body, although the first six were fitted with top-slider ventilators of the type known as the 'Tilling-style', No 6382 onwards featuring the familiar ECW top-radiused metal slider, as apparent on Lowestoft products from the K of 1947 through to the double-deck bodies of the early 1980s.

So when I first met BH&D it would have been fair to say that it was a well-mixed fleet, a kind of bus-liquorice-allsorts! There were AECs with bodywork by Beadle, BH&D, Dodson, Eastern Coach Works and Tilling plus assorted ECOC/ECW-bodied Bristols, Dennis double and single-deckers and, eight AEC 661T trolleybuses with Weymann bodywork, the fleet totalling somewhere around the 150-vehicles mark, plus the ex-WD Canadian Chevrolet tow-truck and the ERF breakdown tender!

Brighton Corporation had been a latecomer to bus operation, despite earlier attempts at such (which were always thwarted by the Thomas Tilling company!). In fact, it was the last municipality to operate only trams, all of which were open-top, and the first buses did not arrive until 1939 when 44 AEC 661T trolleybuses and 21 AEC Regent I 0661 buses were delivered, all 65 vehicles carrying luxuriously-appointed and elegantly-styled Weymann bodywork. The buses were equipped with manually-operated preselector gearboxes plus fluid transmission and 8.8-litre AEC A180F engines as then being fitted concurrently to the London Transport fleet of AEC Regal 10T10 Green Line coaches. Of the 21 Brighton Regents the intent had been to fit ten with bodies by the local builder Thomas Harrington, but its Church Street, Brighton factory was such that double-deckers could not exit the premises and thus the whole order went to Weymann; Nos 60-69 carrying all-metal bodies while those fitted to Nos 70-80 were of composite construction.

In 1947 BCT received a further eight AEC Regents, Mk III 0961 with fluid transmission and air-operated preselector gearboxes plus handsome Weymann bodies, which were an update of the Nos 60-80 styling but being of four-bay construction and numbered 81-88.

Which brings one to the largest of the Brighton-based operators, Southdown Motor Services Ltd. And here I will crave the indulgence of the reader in curbing somewhat (or attempting to …) my Southdown recollections not because of senility and attendant recall-failure but because of the excellent article by Michael H. C. Baker in Buses Extra 78 and my piece in Buses Extra 36 , both of which dealt in some depth with Southdown.

Above: Nine new trolleybuses took to the streets of Brighton during 1948, all of which were BUT 9611T chassis with Weymann 54-seat bodies. The Corporation received six (Nos 45-50) and the remainder became BH&D Nos 6391-3. All nine were withdrawn by stage 1 of the town's trolleybus conversion programme, with seven going to Bournemouth and two to Bradford. No 45 is seen in its Brighton heyday, at Old Steine. Michael Dryhurst

Right: Southdown had a number of its early Titan TD1 and TD2 buses rebodied during the War with austerity specification East Lancs bodies. When the Titans were withdrawn their chassis were scrapped but the bodies went on to assorted utility Guys, such as this example seen in Worthing in 1958. Michael Dryhurst

Relaxed austerity

At that time, SMS had recently received a 25-vehicle batch of Titan PD1 Leylands which carried Park Royal bodies of relaxed austerity style to the Southdown postwar standard configuration of H54R, and these buses were delivered with dark green-painted radiator shells and roofs, which latter had been a wartime precaution against aerial spotting by enemy aircraft. Additionally, the first postwar single-deckers were PS1 Tigers, on which were mounted Eastern Coach Works rear-entrance bus-style bodies, but fitted with coach seats and used exclusively then on the company's London services from the various south coast towns in its area (plus Gosport, which wasn't!). Interestingly, the opening windows on these vehicles were fitted with the previously-mentioned ECW standard top sliding vent, but almost immediately were converted by SMS to pinch-grip half-drops and it was to be another ten years before Southdown took delivery of buses equipped fully with sliding vents.

As, in 1946, the Brighton Corporation fleet was but seven years old, no rebodying had taken place nor was required, despite the fact that with lesser traffic both trolleybuses and motorbuses had been wartime loans to other operators, mostly in areas of much Luftwaffe activity. On the other hand, BH&D and Southdown had embarked on large programmes of rebodying, each starting such ventures in the later years of the war, although BH&D had rebodied some of its Tilling STs with new open-top enclosed-staircase bodies for use on the famous 17 Sea Front Service when it was introduced in 1936. However, 1944 onwards saw further 661-type Regents rebodied, either by Beadle or ECW, and although built to austerity specification, neither firm's designs reflected a utility look; at rebodying, the opportunity was taken to convert these buses to oil engines, the majority receiving Gardner 5LW units, although the AEC 7.7 was fitted to a few.

If my memory serves me correctly Southdown's programme commenced when a number of early TD1 and TD2 Titans had their original bodies replaced by new ones of austerity specification built by East Lancs, followed by some TD3s in the 9xx series. Thereafter, a full rebuild took place of the TD3, TD4 and TD5 fleets, the great majority of these buses being fitted with brand-new bodywork which was supplied by a number of different firms — Beadle, East Lancs, Park Royal, Northern Counties and Saunders. All of these buses were to highbridge layout, the initial Beadle bodies being of six-bay construction, later revised to five-bay styling. No new lowbridge bodies were built on these TD-series chassis, although the remaining lowbridge buses had their existing bodies rebuilt; all SMS lowbridge buses were withdrawn by 1954. BH&D had but a dozen utility buses whereas Southdown took delivery of 100 austerity Guy Arabs, of both Mk I and Mk II versions; the majority of these Guys were Northern Counties-bodied, but units were supplied also by Park Royal, Strachans and Weymann. When the chassis of the rebodied TDl and TD2 buses were scrapped, their East Lancs bodies went on to most of the early Guys, in the main replacing the Strachans units.

In addition to the postwar rebodying of its Leyland TD fleet (I think only one single-decker was rebodied; TS-Tiger bus No 1443 received a new Harrington coach body after war damage), Southdown took delivery of many new vehicles, both buses and coaches. The Park Royal PD1s were followed by 25 similar chassis but with Leyland bodies, and in 1948 came the famous 'JCD' PD2 Titans with H54R Leyland bodies, of which there were 80, numbered 316-95H. Concurrent with these PD2s was a dozen Guys, Nos 500-11H, Mk III Arabs fitted with Northern Counties bodies.

Largest operator

Although there were still many prewar vehicles within the coach fleet (Southdown was for many years the largest operator of coaches in Britain), new stock also featured here. Standardising on the less-powerful Leyland Tiger PS1 chassis, SMS received examples with coachwork by Beadle, Duple, Harrington, Park Royal and Windover plus the aforementioned ECW-bodied machines, all of which represented a huge investment in rolling stock.

Between 1946 and 1950, BH&D took delivery of 40 Bristols with ECW H56R bodywork and of these seven were the K6B variant the rest being the K5G, which struck me always as an odd choice given the very hilly nature of the Brighton area, a factor presumably which influenced the Corporation in its choice of the 8.8 AEC engine for its initial bus fleet rather than specifying the then 1939 AEC standard, the 7.7.

Shortly after the Corporation had received its 0961 Regents, it took delivery of six new trolleybuses, which were BUT 9611T models (the electric equivalent of the AEC Regent III) and although bodied by Weymann these buses were of five-bay construction. As part of the 1938 Act, BH&D was to operate a proportion of the trolleybus mileage, for which work it had taken delivery in 1939 of Nos 6340-7, AEC 661T buses broadly similar to the virtually-identical 44 Corporation trolleybuses; however, these BH&D trolleybuses were stored immediately and did not enter service until 1946/47 with the installing of overhead between Race Hill and Black Rock, the

Left: An unusual Southdown buy was the brace of Bedford OB coaches with standard Duple Vista bodywork, Nos 70/1, the latter being seen here on Madiera Drive, Brighton, one late winter's day in 1954. No 70 formed the basis of a 1:50 scale Corgi Toys (very) limited edition, an example of which now costs something approaching the price of these 1:1 models when new! Michael Dryhurst

Below left: In 1948 Brighton Hove & District built three double-deck bodies in its own workshops at Hove, these ECW-derived designs being mounted on to buses Nos 6245, 6325 and 6338. Seen here at the Fishersgate terminus of route 6 is No 6245 carrying its new BH&D body; note the slight vee-front, built-up wings and flared skirt. The bus was also equipped with fluorescent interior lighting. Michael Dryhurst

BH&D trolleybus working route 44, Seven Dials to Black Rock. BH&D trolleybuses at this time worked on seasonal 43 Old Steine — Black Rock, 43A Old Steine-Race Hill and the 44 routes, and in 1948 were joined by additional trolleybuses Nos 6391-3, similar to BCT Nos 45-50 in being BUT 9611T with Weymann bodies. At this time the other trolleybus services were all Corporation-worked, being: 26 Old Steine-Ditchling Road-Hollingbury (Golf Links), 26A Old Steine-Preston Drove, 40B Old Steine-Brighton Station (seasonal), 41 Queens Park Circular via Lewes Road, 42 Queens Park Circular via Station and 48 Old Steine-Barracks, Lewes Road (an interesting aside is the fact that whenever Corporation buses were running-in at night back to the depot they always displayed '48 Barracks Lewes Rd' irrespective of where they were starting such journeys). With the exception of the crosstown 44, all Brighton trolleybus routes served Old Steine (always referred to on BCT blinds as 'Aquarium, Old Steine'), with the 26/26A/40B /43/43A/46/46A and 48 all terminating at stands on the south end of Old Steine; although there was overhead on the link road by the War Memorial allowing clockwise workings of routes 41/42 to proceed directly from St James' Street to Electricity House, these routes circled Old Steine, the War Memorial overhead later being taken down.

Of the 34 BH&DT services operating in 1947, only six (routes 6, 8, 14, 19, 38, and 44) did not use Old Steine.

Honeypot

And (by my memory count!) of the 25 Southdown bus routes that ran into Brighton all passed through Old Steine as they made their way into the adjacent Pool Valley, the company's principal Brighton terminus, the only SMS exceptions to this terminal being the 12 group, which ran up to the station and beyond, and the 13E/13F/13G Moulscoomb services, which terminated at stands on the west side of Old Steine. Even the Southdown express services traversed Old Steine as they headed for the Steine Street coach station.

Left: In 1956 for a princely six bob (30p) you could take an afternoon excursion on this 'cockroach' and sample the delights of West Sussex with stops at Arundel Castle and Houghton Bridge for tea. Long before the Chalk Pits Museum was even a dream, Amberley was a favoured destination for the Brighton coach operators. This Leyland Comet with Harrington dorsal fin body was No 25 in the fleet of Unique Coaches, Brighton.
Michael Dryhurst

So now you know why so many photographs of buses in Brighton were taken in Old Steine… it was the honeypot of Brighton's bus scene.

And besides the local 'Big Three' a number of other operators served the town, and being a seaside resort it is natural that a number of coach companies were based in Brighton. I recall Alpha Coaches of Ditchling Road and Campings, who were based somewhere behind Lewes Road in the area of The Level; and Unique Coaches, which company's garage was at the top of Trafalgar Street, almost under Brighton station. And all that sticks out in the memory of Alpha rolling stock (and probably so because they were so unusual) were the two normal-control Austins (K3s?) on which were mounted Whitson coachwork in the company's cream and brown livery. Campings had a wonderfully-varied fleet, including the ubiquitous Bedfords OB and SB, Commers Avenger and Commando and AEC, including a 1938 Regal with Harrington dorsal fin body and a Regal III, also with Harrington coachwork, all of which vehicles looked fine in their light blue and cream livery. With the proprietor a former employee of Southdown it is not surprising that the livery of Unique Coaches was two-tone green and cream, nor that at this time they had in stock a couple of normal-control Tilling-Stevens B10B coaches ex-SMS, one of which lasted to the end of the 1953 season; other Unique vehicles were the (un-unique!) Bedford OB and SB, to be joined later by a Harrington-bodied CPO1 Leyland Comet. All of these Brighton coach operators touted for business on Madeira Drive, between the Volk's Railway station and the Palace Pier; further east of here was (is) Peter Pan's Playground where one of the rides was 'Johnstone's Midget Coaches', on which plied perfectly scaled-down replicas of Southdown coaches. Powered by Villiers two-stroke lawnmower engines they carried two passengers, one aft and one behind the driver, and operated on a figure of eight circuit, which was replete with scaled traffic lights and pedestrian crossings marked with belisha beacons. The earliest examples were built completely by Ernie Johnstone in 'The Forge' in Preston Village but

Left: During this period the other major stage carriage operator working regularly into Brighton was Maidstone & District on routes 119/119A joint with Southdown. The usual M&D offerings were one of the Kent operator's immediate postwar standard double-decker, the Bristol K6A with Weymann bodywork; seen here is No DH257, laying over in Pool Valley before returning to Tunbridge Wells. One thing about these buses that sticks in the memory is the fact that the stanchions and handgrabs were ochre-coloured — tres contemporary et tres pre-DiPTAC!
Michael Dryhurst

Top: Regular visitors to Brighton were the East Kent 1950 Dennis Lancet J3 coaches that were fitted with 32-seat Park Royal coach bodies of decidedly dated appearance. No 595 takes a breather at Steine Street, Brighton, after having worked in from Margate on a South Coast Express 'short'. Michael Dryhurst

Middle: Together with East Kent and Southdown, the other participant on the South Coast Express was Western National's Royal Blue, and typical of the vehicles provided was No 1249, a Bristol LL6B with Beadle bodywork incorporating a roof luggage rack, which can just be seen poking up above the roof. The coach is seen in Grand Junction Road, Brighton, heading west for Bournemouth. If one went by the background cars one could be forgiven for thinking the photo was taken in the 1930s rather than 1953! Michael Dryhurst

Bottom: Brighton Corporation received its final AEC buses in the spring of 1950 when Nos 89-94 were delivered; these were Regent III 9612Es with classical Weymann bodies. Replete with semaphore trafficators, No 91 turns at Downsway, the Southwick terminus of route 7. Michael Dryhurst

in the late 1940s he built the chassis and the bodies were built by Harringtons of Hove, who sold them commercially. Built by Johnstone was a total of 57 single-deckers plus a 'tin-fronted' (in 1950!) double-decker registered KCD 1 and painted in the livery of Brighton Corporation which was rebuilt subsequently as a single-decker. Other Johnstone vehicles were six single-decker self-drive buses, two fire engines plus a railway locomotive and tender. Surviving still are a number of these coaches, possibly the best-known being that which graces the top of the Dorchester offices of Bere Regis & District; many were exported, to Australia and the United States, although the majority were to Egypt, particularly Cairo.

All of the Johnstone Brighton 'fleet' carried legal registration-plate numbers, one of the earliest being DUF 3, which was based on a Harrington-bodied Leyland Tiger TS6 of Southdown.

Up on the cliffs at Ovingdean is St Dunstan's, a home for blind ex-servicemen and this institution owned a couple of Harrington-bodied coaches, an Albion Victor and then a Daimler.

Other operators

Which brings us back to the other operators who worked into the town on a regular year-round basis, the distinction being made because during the summer season a multitude of companies' vehicles were to be seen in Brighton. Maidstone & District ventured in from Tunbridge Wells on the jointly-worked (with Southdown) 119/119A, the usual offerings here being invariably the postwar M&D standard, the Bristol K6A with Weymann bodywork, but occasionally one of the Saunders-

Right: This is one of the Harrington-bodied Johnstone Midget Coaches, in Southdown livery but carrying a 'Guy' nameplate; although fitted with a tonneau, the driving position would be about where the word 'Museum' is, and passengers sit aft and forward of there. This example is seen in Rolvenden, Kent, outside a small motor museum. (That's a small museum for motors, rather than ... mind you, it could be correct.) Roger Knight

Right: The 'Ron Glum' of coach designs ... . In 1951 Southdown received its first underfloor-engined vehicles with the delivery of Nos 800-9, which were Leyland Royal Tigers with Duple 41-seat centre-entrance bodies obviously derived from the Vega design. These coaches were painted all over one-tone green and not (in the opinion of the writer) to good effect. Originally No 808, but renumbered by the time of this summer 1963 photo, No 1808 passes through Midhurst. Michael Dryhurst

Right: At the end of the 1951 season the stalwart Brush-bodied Leyland Titan TD1s were withdrawn by Southdown. Apart from temporary covering to the top decks of some of these buses during World War 2, they were open-topped, outside-staircased and petrol-engined for the whole of their working lives from 1929-51. This is No 813 seen in Old Steine in May 1950; the bus has long been preserved by the Southdown company. Michael Dryhurst

bodied K6As would appear. Another joint operation was the South Coast Express, at its fullest extent, a Bournemouth to Margate service involving East Kent (Park Royal-bodied coaches, either PS1 Tigers or Dennis Lancet J3s), Royal Blue (Bristol L6B/Beadle) and Southdown, usually Beadle or Duple PS1s. And in the summer came the hordes of excursion coaches from London and

Top: To replace the Brush-bodied Titans Southdown converted a number of utility Guys into permanent open-toppers, the styling of which resembled BH&D practice. This is No 444, seen at Southwick when working the 34-mile long Arundel-Devil's Dyke service 102, at the time reputedly the longest open-top route in the UK.
Michael Dryhurst

Middle: Campings Coaches was another Brighton operator offering excursions and tours and, although it operated a number of Bedfords and Commers, the fleet also included some 'heavyweights', all of which were AECs. This Regal IV 9821E with Gurney Nutting centre-entrance bodywork was an exhibit at the 1952 Earls Court Commercial Motor Show.
Michael Dryhurst

Bottom: Southdown received the last of its Farington-style Leyland-bodied PD2/12 Titans in 1953, having taken 54 such bodies over the previous two years; seen here is the very last, No 754. By the time of this photograph in 1963 the bus had received the modified Southdown livery introduced in 1957 whereby the area of cream around the upper deck was reduced and the dark green lining-out discontinued. The bus is seen heading into Brighton from Haywards Heath, at London Road, Withdean.
Michael Dryhurst

the surrounding Home Counties, plus the vehicles of companies providing extended tours many of which based tours on Brighton or used it as a one or two day stopover; I recall a Lancashire operator by the name of Robinson, with a very attractive green livery being a familiar sight in the town during the summer months.

Of the seasonal daily excursion vehicles, those that stand out particularly in the memory are the varied coaches that were hired by London Transport for use as relief buses on weekdays which came to the coast at weekends, complete with LT badges and route details, and of LT vehicles themselves. As a youngster it was a ritual for me to stand out on Preston Road and watch the crowds of coaches descending on the town and one Sunday morning in June 1950 this 12-year-old was astonished to see three RTs come flashing towards him, two Central Area buses and green RT623 from Hemel Hempstead. From that time RTs and RTLs became regular visitors, but I do not ever recall seeing an RTW on coastal excursion work. Did they undertake such duties?

Once in Brighton and having dropped the punters off on Madeira Drive, the visitor vehicles headed for parking; the independents usually used the large municipal coach park at Whitehawk or the lesser ones at Edward Street and Russell Street or even at the bottom of Hove Street, Hove,

Top: Being set in its double-deck ways, Southdown was not a natural target for demonstrators, although in July 1954 this very interesting bus was on trial. It was the first rear-engined Leyland Lowloader prototype, STF 90, the forerunner of the Atlantean. It had a Saunders low-height rear-entrance body with open rear platform, on the rear wall of which sat the O.350 Leyland engine, and access to the driver's cab was via a sliding door fitted to the front bulkhead. Whether intentional or not, the bus was painted in Southdown's green and cream scheme, and it is seen here at the Tongdean Lane, Brighton, terminus of route 12 on which it spent all of its Southdown time.
Michael Dryhurst

Middle: During 1957 the Hastings Tramways fleet was integrated fully with that of parent company Maidstone & District. The integration included the wearing of M&D fleetnames and livery, *sans* aluminium-painted roof, and No 34 is seen here after such treatment. Note that the fully-informative destination display allows no room for a route number, so instead this is carried in the driver's windscreen; so what's new? A Sunbeam W with Weymann bodywork, the trolleybus was part of a batch of vehicles delivered in 1947/48, and with five others it was subsequently sold to Maidstone Corporation.
Michael Dryhurst

Bottom: With the virtual standardisation on the Bristol Lodekka by ex-Tilling companies after 1954, BH&D was the exception in continuing adherence to the highbridge 'K' series. However, in 1957 Bristol discontinued the model, BH&D No 500 being the last of a very long line. Interestingly, these last eight BH&D buses were 7ft 6in wide KS6G models with 62-seat bodies, all of which initially went on to route 14. Note the louvres over the side windows, a feature peculiar to some of BH&D's 'K' series buses, to reappear subsequently on many of the company's Lodekkas.
Michael Dryhurst

while vehicles allied with BET, BTC or the London Transport fleets parked-up in the BH&D Whitehawk garage. For some reason, Aldershot & District eschewed this arrangement and parked in the forecourt of the former Kemp Town railway station.

In those days, the complete Brighton Corporation fleet was housed and maintained in the former tram depot on Lewes Road (as today are the vehicles of its successor, Brighton Buses). Brighton, Hove & District had its main works and garage near Hove station at Conway Street (as does today's B&H) plus the large garage at Whitehawk on Brighton's eastern extremity, where the 11-vehicle BH&D trolleybus fleet was also based. The principal Southdown garage in the locality was at Edward Street across from the Royal Pavilion while the main works of SMS, although some distance from any Southdown bus route were at least plumb in the centre of the company's operating area, at Portslade.

Eventful year

1950 was a fairly eventful year within the Brighton bus scene, insomuch as BH&D had on hire the second prototype Bristol Lodekka, West Yorkshire DX1, and the AEC Regent IV underfloor-engined double-decker paid a visit to the town, although not seeing any public service here while running on trade plate 316I I. The Corporation took delivery of some more Regent III, this time 9612E models with Weymann bodywork, numbered 89-94, and to the company came Bristol K5Gs Nos 6400-6 (EAP 8-11, EPM 1-3), which were late deliveries having been on hire to LTE for nearly a year, at Tottenham garage. These seven buses were odd in that they had solid wooden seat grabs, harking back to utility practice.

The BH&D Dennis Lances were despatched to Westcliff-on-Sea Motor Services, having first been converted to open top by BH&D. In fact, BH&D undertook considerable maintenance and bodywork repairs for other Tilling group operators, particularly Tilling's Transport (BTC) Ltd, Westcliff and the Lincolnshire Road Car Co., a number of which company's Bristol K6A/Park Royal utility buses were rebuilt at Hove.

Above: Given the amount of traffic it handled, especially in the summer months, Southdown's Steine Street, Brighton, coach station was extremely cramped as can be judged here, the entrance being immediately behind the Tiger Cub/Beadle hiding shyly behind the pillar. It was unusual for Southdown to hire coaches from local operators but it was the case on this occasion with a Thurgood-bodied Bedford SB of Billingshurst Coaches assigned as a relief car on the South Coast Express. Michael Dryhurst

Southdown had an exhibit at the 1950 Earls Court Commercial Motor Show, being vehicle No 700H, a Leyland Titan PD2/12 on to which was mounted a Northern Counties FHC50RD (fully-fronted-highbridge-coach-seating 50-with-an-enclosed doored-rear-entrance…) body of four-bay construction, the only four-bay 'decker ever owned by SMS. The vehicle was intended for the Eastbourne — London service, on which it was used only irregularly.

At the end of 1950 the first eight-footers arrived for BH&D when in the closing days of the year buses Nos 6427-9 were delivered to Hove; these were KSW6B Bristols with handsome H60R bodies by Eastern Coach Works.

On the Brighton scene in 1951 the fabulous Faringtons arrived, when both Maidstone & District and Southdown placed in service buses fitted with the handsome Leyland bodies based on the Titan PD2/12. The M&D order consisted of both highbridge and lowbridge versions while SMS Nos 701-724H were H58R with matching KUF registrations; both the M&D and SMS buses were subsequently fitted with enclosed platforms. Also in 1951 Southdown received its first underfloor-engined vehicles, Leyland Royal Tiger PSU1/15 numbered 801-10 with 41-seat centre-entrance coachwork by Duple of a distinctly 'glum' look, in a revised (and not for the better…) livery of all-over Southdown green. I thought they were 'orrible. The fleet of PS1 coaches continued the prewar coach livery of dark green roof, wings and lower body trim with Southdown green bodywork relieved by a yellow flash, but all of the initial Royal Tiger coaches, both Duple and Harrington were in this new livery, and, in fact, the PS1s were painted into it during overhauls in the mid-1950s.

The 26A/46A BH&DT trolleybus services were, in fact, a circular route, Old Steine-Preston Drove-Old Steine; on reaching Preston Drove a clockwise 46A would change blinds to '26A' and continue then via Ditchling Road back to Old Steine. Likewise leaving Old Steine as an anti-clockwise 26A, this would change to a 46A and work back via Beaconsfield Road (for some odd reason when laying-over at Preston Drove, clockwise workings did so at Five Ways, anti-clockwise buses opposite Balfour Road). Work had been proceeding apace on wiring the 'Outer Circle' in which the 26 was extended northwards to the junction of Carden Hill, while the 46 was extended via Surrenden Road, Braybon Avenue and Carden Avenue to Carden Hill, at which point it became a 26, and vice versa. The Hollingbury outer circle was opened to traffic in September 1951, taking trolleybuses through many of the Corporation's postwar housing and light industrial estates, this being the final trolleybus extension, and, but three years later were heard the first mutterings in public about replacing the trolleybuses with motorbuses.

Varied fleet

The other Sussex municipal operator was (is) Eastbourne Corporation, the composition of which fleet could not be of greater contrast to that of Brighton; in the early 1950s ECT was operating TD1, TD2, TD4, PD1 and PD2 Titans, AEC Regents of marks I, II and III, Crossley DD42, AEC Regal III, and Leyland Lion LT9! Not bad for a relatively small fleet of fewer than 60 vehicles… And bodywork was varied too, being by Bruce, East Lancs, Leyland, Northern Counties and Weymann. The livery was dark blue and deep yellow, with a rich cream roof. Eastbourne did not take delivery of its first oil-engined bus until 1946 and so in the early 1950s the LT9 , TD4s and Regent Is had their petrol units replaced by Leyland 8.6-litre oil engines, which I think came from scrapped Southdown vehicles.

Southdown, of course, had a large presence in Eastbourne, and M&D buses were also to be seen here, working on joint routes 15 and 99, between the town and Hastings.

The latter town boasted the only other Sussex trolleybus system, although this was not a municipal venture, the Hastings Tramways Co. being a subsidiary of M&D since 1935. Again, as the activities of this company have been chronicled most excellently in CB4 , I'll say little else, except that when I made the acquaintance of this fleet first, the trolleybuses had green-painted roofs and carried the fleetname 'Hastings Tramways' emblazoned impressively across the front lower panels, as well as on the vehicle sides.

Hastings is where, in those days, one encountered some stage services of the East Kent Road Car Co, to Pett and Rye (and Ashford?), and in my time they were all single-deck operated and in the hands of the CFN-registered Dennis Lancet J3s, which carried Park Royal rear-entrance bodies. And again M&D ran into Hastings; in fact, it was the major operator here. And didn't the little East Sussex independent Dengate or Northiam have services into Hastings? I recall seeing his OWBs here…

Ungainly and underpowered

But back to Brighton. More buses came to BH&D in March of 1951 in the shape of Nos 6419-26, which were somewhat ungainly by carrying on their 90in wide Bristol KS chassis bodies of 96in width; also they were powered (if that is the apposite word in this context) by Gardner 5LW engines. And all the time, elderly AEC Regents and then Bristol GO5Gs were being withdrawn. In 1952 came Nos 6430-6. Bristol KSW6B/H60R, but very soon thereafter the last bus received a 6LW engine to become 'KSW6G', to be followed by 56 similar buses over the next four years. Some second-hand additions arrived in 1953 when five Duple-bodied K6A Bristols were purchased from London Transport, one bus (ex-B28) being sold-on immediately. These buses initiated a new BH&D numbering series when they became Nos 5996-9 (ex-B22/18/19/29), and in 1955 new ECW H60R bodies were fitted to the quartet. Further second-hand buses arrived in 1955 when several 1939/40 Bristol K5Gs were purchased from Bristol (was it 'Omnibus' by then or still 'Tramways'?); in due course these buses were rebuilt by BH&D to convertible open-top configuration receiving PV2 radiators and wings at the same time, the same process having been accorded to BH&D's own 1940 Bristols, Nos 6348-62.

BH&D rebuilt all of its Park Royal-bodied Bristols in 1952/3, which treatment included the fitting of rear destination screens; at the same time Nos 6371/2/3 received Gardner 5LW units in place of their AEC 7.7s, and then some interesting body swaps occurred.

In 1948, BH&D had built three bodies in its own shops; although to the basic ECW design, they had a distinctive Brighton, rather than Lowestoft, look, and each body was equipped with different features. That put on to Regent No 6245 had built-up front wings and fluorescent interior lighting, that on GO5G No 6325 had standee windows fitted above the three main lower-deck bays and K5G No 6338's body sported direction indicators fitted either side of the front and rear destination screens, but never used because of local police objections. However, as the Regent and GO5G chassis were scrapped the bodies moved to the CPM utilities; minus the built-up front wings, the No 6245 body went on to No 6370 and that from No 6325 to No 6372. But when K5G No 6336 was scrapped, its Tilling-style BH&D body was saved, widened between the bulkheads, fitted with a 'new look' front (fibreglass not tin!) but retaining its Tilling outline six-bay construction and placed on to… No 6372. In 1954 Nos 6374/5 had their Park Royal bodies replaced by new H60R ECW units, at the same time becoming K5Gs.

Other significant withdrawals not mentioned previously were of the Southdown 800-series Titans (TD1 not PD3!), which had retained their petrol engines and open-top Brush bodies right from 1929 to 1951, these being replaced on seasonal services by converting to open-top configuration a number of the Mk II Arabs. Also, Brighton Corporation found itself embarrassingly 'over-bussed' to the extent that the newest Regent III buses were used only seasonally and then stored in a covered market near Brighton Town Hall! To remedy this bizarre situation it was decided to sell the composite-constructed Regents, and Nos 70-80 departed to a Cardiff dealer in late summer 1952.

Southdown took another 20 PD2/12 Faringtons in 1952 (Nos 725-44H), PSU1/15 Royal Tigers with both Duple and Harrington coachwork plus, for London express duties and lengthy cross-country work, 25 PSU1/15 Royal Tigers fitted with Leyland C41C bodies. And there were also the first large-capacity single-decker buses for some 14 years; these 10 (Nos 1500-9) also were Royal Tigers, model PSU1/13, fitted with East Lancs rear-entrance bodies and thus were crew-operated. Always to these eyes heavy-looking buses, these were followed in 1953 by a further 30 PSU1/13s, with no-less bulky B40C East Lancs bodies.

Ultimately, all of the SMS Royal Tiger buses were converted to front entrance, for OMO. The final batch of Faringtons were the 10 received in early 1953, and were the last Southdown double-deckers to have hinged cab doors; these were followed by another 10 PD2/12s in the summer, which carried very good-looking NCME bodies equipped with sliding cab doors. It should be pointed out also that buses from No 725H onwards were delivered with enclosed platforms. These latter Titans were the last new 'deckers for two years.

Beadles

In company with East Kent and M&D (and a number of other BET companies plus Birch Bros), Southdown took delivery in 1952 of some Beadle 'semi-chassisless' coaches, in this instance based on Tiger TS-series engines and components built to 30ft x 8ft dimensions, incorporating a full-front and centre door, but as Southdown still was not enamoured with sliding vents, these rebuilds were fitted with half-drop windows. And they were followed a year later by another batch, albeit to a shorter length and featuring deeper windscreens and a forward entrance.

Further underfloor-engined coaches were PSU1/15 Nos 1645-9, which carried heavy-looking C41C Duple bodies of the builder's 'Coronation' style, followed by Nos 1650-9, again by Duple but to a less-bulky look, similar coaches following in 1954. However, 'lightweight' was the heavy word of the times and after having employed a Leyland Tiger Cub demonstrator in the Worthing area SMS took delivery in 1954 of 20 PSUC1/1 chassis which were fitted with Duple Midland B39F bodies built in the former Nudd Bros & Lockyer factory; these buses featured a mix of quarter-drop and top-slider windows — a Southdown first — ventilation progress here! Presumably, the siting of the passenger door was the reason that both batches of the previous Royal Tiger buses had offside cab doors, which were hinged, and although built as front-entrance buses these Tiger Cubs also had an offside cab door, albeit of the sliding type.

As an aside, Southdown has always been — wrong tense, Dryhurst, was! — an interesting company especially with its vehicle-purchasing policy whereby at times one could be forgiven for questioning if the company was actually part of the BET group. By the mid-1950s the BET standard saloon was the AEC Reliance or the Leyland Tiger Cub; okay, SMS had never been an AEC user, but now had 20 Tiger Cub buses. However, the BET PSUC1/1 norm carried bodywork either by Saunders, Weymann or Willowbrook. Not Southdown though. And by now the MCW Orion body was commonplace in most BET fleets. Not Southdown though. And a number of BET companies was specifying the 'new look' PD2/20 Titan, but not-you-know-who! I mean, just look at Southdown's next intake of coaches over the three-year period 1954-57 — 130 Tiger Cubs, 25 Beadle-Commer T48B integrals and three Royal Tigers. All right, you might say, nothing odd there... except that all of the PSUC1/2 coaches carried Beadle coachwork (of a very bland style), 115 of which were to a basic C41C layout, the remainder with front-entrance bodies; I think the Beadle integral was bought only by three other BET companies and then only in penny numbers and the three 1955 Royal Tigers (the last of the breed for SMS) were model PSU1/11 with Harrington bodies not of the then Hove coachbuilders contemporary style per the M&D Reliances, but of the 1952 'heavy' look! Whereas Tiger Cub coaches in other BET fleets were usually fitted with bodies by Burlingham or Willowbrook, with a sprinkling of Duple's Donington, and the emerging Weymann Fanfare, but Beadle?

And of course, Southdown's double-decker policy wasn't exactly BET mainstream. Having had on demonstration in 1954 the prototype PDR1 Leyland rear-engined Low-loader, SMS did not commit to a rear-engined double-decker for another 15 years and then only by virtue of Hobson's choice, in the interim having built-up a fleet of over 200 PD3 Titans, which the company purchased right into the mid-1960s. Funnily enough, BET neighbour East Kent pursued a similar policy with its AEC Regent V standard, that rotten Hobson again dictating Fleetlines in cahoots with Barbara Castle!

Idiosyncratic

Not that the other two Brighton operators weren't idiosyncratic. Despite using a demonstrator Daimler CD650/Roe in March 1952, Brighton Corporation did not acquire any buses from 1950 until 1959, although in February 1953 it did place into service two BUT 9611T trolleybuses with Weymann bodies (Nos 51/52), the chassis of which had been purchased some few years earlier, and while BH&D had operated prototype Lodekka buses in both 1950 and 1953 (Western National No 1863) the Company did not purchase any of the type until 1959, the last ex-Tilling operator to do so, having standardised on the KS-series until 1957 when the model was discontinued by Bristol Commercial Vehicles.

With the entry into service of the large fleets of Royal Tiger and Tiger Cub vehicles, all Southdown prewar single-deckers had by now disappeared, including the wonderful 1400-series Harrington-bodied Tiger buses, many of which had metamorphosed into the Beadle rebuilds, and the ECW-bodied Tigers had been cascaded to bus work. All of the utility Guys had been rebuilt, the most conspicuous feature being that all roof domes had been 'rounded off', while some were now open-toppers.

With BH&D all of the GO5G Bristols had gone, as had most of the AECs, the only Regents remaining with the company being a handful of open-toppers, which came off after the 1956 season.

Which seems a suitable juncture at which to terminate these reminiscences, because shortly thereafter came a whole new Sussex scene — trolleybus withdrawals and the eventual abandonment of the two systems, at Hastings (1959) and Brighton (1961) and then the creation of Brighton Area Transport Services, the triumvirate of BCT, BH&D and SMS, taking red buses into new areas such as Saltdean and Shoreham and Southdown buses on to Brighton town services. And Brighton Corporation forsaking AEC and standardising on the Leyland PD2 for its motorbus orders, and even buying second-hand TD5s from Southdown. But that story must wait.
Another time, perhaps... ?

In conclusion I would like to thank my old friend Alan Platt of Brighton for checking my notes and also for enlarging on them where necessary, particularly with regard to 'Johnstone's Midget Coaches.'

Below: As with seaside resorts up and down the land, Brighton was host to a wonderful variety of visiting coaches. This is the first Rutland Clipper rear-engined R6 coach, which was sold initially to the West Kent Motor Services of H. W. Crouch, Biggin Hill, in 1954 and subsequently to Spiers' of Henley-on-Thames, in which ownership it is seen here in the summer of 1958. Coachwork was by Whitson of West Drayton. Michael Dryhurst

Classic Bus Alphabet/3

P IS FOR POLE. Poles are useful things for which to attach bus stops, but if you're a trolleybus, poles have all sorts of uses. If you're well-versed in these things, then the things that stick out of the top of a trolleybus, and mark it out from being a motorbus, are called booms. If you're not, poles does just as well. Trolleybuses rely on the juxtaposition of these poles to the wires, to maintain traction, and therefore the wires are held up by traction poles. If you drive your trolleybus too fast over the points (another P, note, but again if you know your trolleybuses, for some reason you would call them 'frogs') your poles would go 'Poing', fly up in the air and the whole shooting match would grind to a halt.

On the continent they have cissy things called pole retrievers, a high-tech device comprising a long piece of string. Not so here. The conductor would dive off the platform, grovel under the bus and, so long as nothing had stopped within about 25ft of the back of it, would produce another pole, this time of bamboo, with a hook on the end;would point it skywards and wave it around a bit till the trolleypoles were restored to their contact with the wires (ensuring the right pole was on the right wire, otherwise you have problems with yet another sort of pole altogether; if you got this wrong it caused much hilarity, and was therefore abbreviated to pole-arity) and away you would go. Much more fun than a long piece of string.

Q IS FOR, WELL, Q. There has always been something about the letter Q that was mysterious. AEC, which had previously dealt in Regals, Regents, Reliances and Renowns, chose the designation Q for its revolutionary 1932 side-engined chassis — surely a model that was ahead of its time. And Quest 80 was the name chosen in 1979 for a chassis that was, er... I rest my case.

R IS FOR REAR, where purists argue the platform should always be on a classic bus and the engine should never be. Not to be confused with rare, a quality guaranteed to ensure that any such vehicle is automatically a classic, even if its engine is at the rear and its entrance isn't.

S IS FOR SEDDON — remember them? They made little Perkins-powered buses and coaches in the early postwar boom, basing them on modified truck chassis. Then they tried again in the 1960s, selling small numbers of coaches.

When rear-engined single-deckers were all the rage they came up

Left: Trolley poles have been added in a rather curious way to this photograph of a West Yorkshire PTE MCW Metrobus to mock-up how the proposed new-generation of trolleybuses might look. Although South Yorkshire PTE went to the length of building a prototype using a Dennis chassis and Alexander body, West Yorkshire contented itself with this photograph.

with the RU (Crosville bought 100), and when the Scottish Bus Group wanted a Gardner-engined Leopard, they built that too, in the shape of the Pennine VII. But surely they'll best be remembered as the inventors of the midibus. When Selnec Passenger Transport Executive wanted to try out small buses, it was to the Oldham-based manufacturer it turned. And out popped the Pennine IV:236. Selnec was the biggest buyer, but other places tried them too — notably Edinburgh, Doncaster and Cardiff corporations.

The little Pennines performed well, but they were ahead of their time. Seddon still builds trucks at Oldham, but is now part of the mighty Iveco group.

Above: What might be regarded as a midibus, a Seddon Pennine IV demonstrator, with Seddon's own Pennine Coachcraft 45-seat bodywork, that was on loan to Halifax Corporation. A later version of the Pennine IV was the basis of the Midi, a phrase apparently coined by Seddon.

T IS FOR TRAM AND FOR TITAN. Now if you were Leyland in the late 1920s, what you wanted was for most of municipal operators to bury the former with the latter. This was the subtle form of advertising which was used in those days to promote your revolutionary new product. For revolutionary the Titan was, and arguably set the standard for double-deckers for almost the next 40 years. It had a sweet, powerful six-cylinder petrol engine, a drop-frame chassis, a choice of lowbridge or highbridge body (see L and H), both of which normally had a roof. Later versions had almost equally sweet diesel engines, proving that not only was a diesel (or oiler, as they were more often called in those days) cheap to run, it needn't rattle your fillings out either. Postwar Leyland carried on building Titans, arguably the finest and most reliable postwar buses of the lot, only ending production in 1968 when the industry was being encouraged by Bus Grant to move to one-man operation.

Below: How it was done. The chassis of the revolutionary 1930s AEC Q, showing the side-mounted engine compartment.

Undoubtedly Leyland's bid to Bury a Tram with a Titan was highly successful. By the end of the 1920s, as well-known tramway historian Ian Yearsley has recently been revealing, municipalities had used up their replacement funds for tramway infrastructure in subsidising the rates, and therefore found themselves with worn-out track and equipment, often still the subject of heavy loans, and no money in the kitty to do anything with them. So they did just that; buried them with Titans. Perhaps in 40 years' time Volvo will come up with a revolutionary new double-decker, call it the Titan, and suggest the good people of Sheffield and Manchester do the same thing again. Because, from what one gathers, the new tramway operators haven't learned the lesson about making provision for future replacement.

THE ROAD FROM SHORT TROUSERS

GAVIN BOOTH remembers the excitement of early discoveries in the 1950s.

PICTURE a gangly youth, probably wearing school uniform right down to regulation grey shorts, standing by the open door of a bus garage looking pathetic, hoping someone will take pity and invite him to take a look inside. Yes, folks — that youth was me in the 1950s, but I suspect that this sad image strikes a chord with many *Yearbook* readers who have been there, maybe at a different time — and probably more suitably dressed.

Change the time, the place, the clothes, and I know from enthusiasts I meet and letters I receive at *Classic Bus* that many of us followed a similar path when we first felt our way into an interest in buses.

Today, when there seem to be few bus stations in Britain without the statutory camera-toting notebook-wielding enthusiast, it is odd to recall a time when you could take an active interest in buses without ever meeting another devotee. It was easy to believe that you were a lone pioneer, furtively pursuing an interest that was, well, odd. Remember that 40 years ago there wasn't the mini-industry that has grown up around bus enthusiasts. There was *Buses Illustrated*, but this didn't have the widespread distribution that *Buses*, its present-day successor, enjoys, and unless you came across it by chance, you might never know it existed. Ian Allan also produced ABCs of major bus fleets — OK if you lived in London, Bristol, Birmingham, Kent or northwest England, but in other parts of the 'provinces' we didn't get a look in. There was the Omnibus Society, of course, and the PSV Circle, and when we eventually joined these organisations we discovered that we were not alone. From that point we were able to compare notes with like-minded individuals, and this helped to broaden our horizons.

Above: The PSV Licence disc on Scottish Omnibuses No B221 told me that it had chassis number 06623588, the radiator told me that it was an AEC Regal, a bakelite plate told me the body was built by Alexander, and a transfer on the rear told me it had seats for 39 passengers. I later found that it dated from 1940, and was one of 20 'short cab' Regals with high-capacity bodies, similar to the more familiar Leyland TS8 Specials favoured by SMT group companies. B221 was in service until 1962, and is seen in St Andrew Square bus station, Edinburgh, in 1959.
All photographs by Gavin Booth

Voyage of discovery

The 1950s was a good time to discover buses. Many fleets still had prewar buses in service, most had some wartime vehicles, and the postwar appetite for new buses meant that they were being swallowed up as fast as the manufacturers could build them and so any attempt at standardisation was often thrown to the four winds.

I suspect that most of us start with our local fleets, quickly building up rudimentary fleetlists that later turned out to be fairly accurate. It was easy for me with Edinburgh Corporation. The buses all ran within the city boundaries, and there was such a concentration in Princes Street and the High Street that few escaped my notice.

Legislation made it a bit easier than it is today: all buses carried PSV Licence discs alongside their tax discs, and these quoted the chassis number. And buses and coaches displayed their seating capacity on the outside. Not only that, but most chassis builders made sure their names were prominently displayed on radiators or front panels. Daimler didn't, but everyone knew what the fluted radiator stood for. Crossley's Maltese cross was more of a mystery until I got close enough to inspect the licence disc.

Of course the subtleties of different type designations weren't so easy. Even if I had known that there were such things as Daimler CVD6s and CVG6s, I wouldn't have known what the differences were; all I knew was that some apparently identical buses sounded different.

Bodybuilders were normally keen to let the world know about their products, so transfers, plastic or metal badges, or gearbox cowlings usually proclaimed at least a name, sometimes a town name, occasionally the information that the body was metal-framed, and patent numbers were not unknown. Northern Counties even told you how often the air was changed in the upper saloon. The trouble was, this information was inside the bus, and required seekers of knowledge to board the bus, perhaps even paying money to a conductor in the process. Prominent plates on the stairs of a double-decker or step risers of a single-decker were fine; they could be read from the pavement. But small transfers or plates mounted on the bulkhead behind the driver presented problems, and inevitably led to gaps in the fleetlists.

Above: A familiar Edinburgh visitor in the 1950s, United No BU184, a 1955 Bristol LS5G with ECW 45-seat bus body, hardly the thing, you might think, for the long joint service to Newcastle, but the nature of the service meant that few people travelled right through. It is seen in the Queen Street, Edinburgh, parking stances.

Further-flung buses

After I thought I had got to grips with the Edinburgh fleet, I turned my attention to the other buses that could be seen in the city. Scottish Omnibuses (SOL), though based in the city, had depots as far away as Berwick and Airdrie, and some of the buses used in these further-flung areas only ventured into Edinburgh for overhaul and repainting. It wasn't just the mild excitement of unfamiliar individual vehicles paying an occasional visit to Edinburgh — there was the unexpected discovery of totally different types which were peculiar to one area. The first sight of one of SOL's five ex-London Guy Arabs, rebuilt as 30ft single-deckers, was greeted with disbelief, and it was some time before I understood the whole story behind them. And there was S1, the home-made integral bus — today we'd call it a midibus — built by SOL in 1956 and based on the Albion Claymore underfloor-engined goods model. This odd little bus, a predecessor of the Nimbus, was banished to Bathgate depot to operate on a hospital service, and rarely strayed

Right: Parked in Market Street, Edinburgh, during its Grand Tour of Britain, is Southdown No 1816, a 1951 Leyland Royal Tiger PSU1/15 with Harrington 26-seat (two-and-one seating) coach body.

Below right: Falkirk bus station could always be relied upon to produce buses of interest. Parked up together in 1960 are two of the well-maintained antiques from the Alexander fleet: No R321 was an unfrozen 1941 all-Leyland Titan TD7, one of 13 delivered that year; No RO471, at the back, was a 1944 Daimler CWA6 with lowbridge Brush body. Both buses passed to the newly-created Alexander (Midland) in 1961 and both were withdrawn in 1963.

outside West Lothian. One advantage of attending a city centre school was the after-school pilgrimages to places of interest. Edinburgh Corporation's Central Garage at Annandale Street was not far away. SOL's head office and main depot were situated in New Street, literally below my school, and Market Street, next to Edinburgh Waverley station, and leading from New Street, was one of the popular parking places for visiting coaches.

At New Street and Annandale Street I would peer pathetically in at the main doors to see what was new. New deliveries at New Street were often parked near the door, so I could add these to my lists, and sometimes a friendly depot inspector would invite me to inspect the latest acquisition. Annandale Street was different. The new vehicles, and any oddments like demonstrators, were parked at the bottom end of the garage, and only tantalising glimpses were possible until I realised that there was a side door that was sometimes open, which allowed much closer inspection.

The visiting coaches provided a taste of fleets that were otherwise only names from BI. Southdown coaches seemed to be the most regular visitors, usually Leyland Royal Tigers with Duple or Harrington bodies, with that plush-looking two-and-one seating. Midland Red coaches were also familiar, strange-looking to eyes used to Burlinghams and Duples, and I remember being amazed to note that the body plate on a C4 announced that it was built in Stirling by

Above: A 45-mile journey to find an Atlantean may seem strange today, but in 1959 there were so few around that many enthusiasts made such trips. Glasgow Corporation No LA1 was one of the first four Leyland Atlantean PDR1/1, exhibited at the 1958 Earls Court Commercial Motor Show. It was the only one of the four with Alexander bodywork, which many felt was more stylish than the more familiar MCW design. The vehicle went on to driver training duties in 1973, and is now preserved.

Below: Although this Laurie, Hamilton, Leyland Titan PD2 looks fairly normal, it is not what it seems. The chassis of HD 7826 was new to Yorkshire Woollen in 1948 and while with Laurie it received this 1939 Leyland body from Birmingham Leyland TD6c, FOF 307. As the Leyland body design changed little from the mid-1930s to 1950, the combination looked quite natural. Behind it in this 1961 view at the Burnbank Road garage, is the rear of a recently-acquired London RTL.

Walter Alexander. Essex County Coaches, liveried as WTA, sent Roe Dalesman-bodied AEC Reliances; Northern General sent Picktree-bodied Guy Arabs, and Ribble sent Burlingham-bodied Royal Tigers.

Ribble was also a regular visitor to the city on joint express services from Lancashire, and while these were most frequently Leyland-bodied Royal Tiger coaches, one of the treats at busy weekends in July and August was to spot the prewar Leyland Tiger TS7s and TS8s rebodied by Duple in 1949/50, running duplicates to Blackpool and Morecambe.

Although they were ostensibly up to 20 years old, they performed well, and were no older than AEC Regals pressed into service by SOL on its share of long-distance services.

United was the other 'foreign' operator to be seen regularly in Edinburgh, first with Bristol L5Gs and then with LS5Gs — YHN 184 was a regular performer for many years. At busy times, United also pressed older vehicles into service, like the olive green and cream-liveried Leyland Tiger TS8s normally found on the Tyne-Tees-Thames services.

A taste for travel

The next stage was to explore further afield. But how? At the age of, say, 15 there were problems to overcome — certainly in the 1950s. Lack of money was one; parental opposition another. But these could be overcome.

One way that worked for me was to convince my parents that they wanted a day out — though it was easier to convince them that we should go to, say, Stirling or Glasgow, than it was to get them to Airdrie or Motherwell, where there were untold excitements waiting to be enjoyed.

But Stirling or Glasgow were fine for starters. Stirling, by bus via Falkirk for the Booths were still car-less at the time, was a revelation. Although Alexanders operated into Edinburgh with fairly up-to-date stock, a bridge at Linlithgow prevented double-deckers from working further east. So I was unprepared for the wealth of elderly buses seen in and around Falkirk, buses that were in some cases to survive for a number of years, some even into the post-1961 Alexander (Midland) business. These glimpses and the tantalising sight of Alexander's sprawling Larbert Road depot made me vow to return.

Glasgow, still very much tram-dominated, was almost too much to take in on brief day visits, particularly when the Argyle Street shops beckoned my parents, but I managed to drag my father through to Shettleston in 1957 to find the two Lowland Leyland PDR1 rear-engined

Top: Sitting, out of service, at Laurie's Hamilton garage was FOF 182, an ex-Birmingham 1939 Daimler COG5 with Metro-Cammell 54-seat body, bought in 1954. Birmingham was a popular source of secondhand buses for Laurie until the London RTLs came on to the market.

Above: Pictured in the Norfolk village of Woodbastwick in 1960, Eastern Counties No A226 was a 1933 Leyland Titan TD2 with Gardner 5LW engine and 1949 ECW lowbridge body. Note the CovRad radiator and the position of the route number.

prototypes — which we duly did — and this turned out to be my only opportunity to see this fascinating fleet — although Lowland buses turning up in Edinburgh in green after the takeover by SOL provided local excitement for some time to come. Not the PDR1s, though — they were sold; the Scottish Bus Group wasn't ready for rear-engined double-deckers, if indeed it ever was.

I was introduced to other fleets almost by accident. We had relatives who moved to Glenboig, of all places, and this meant a tedious trip by bus, usually an SOL AEC Regent III, from Edinburgh to Coatbridge, where we changed on to a bus from the Carmichael's of Glenboig fleet. I say the journey was tedious and would hasten to assure AEC fans that this didn't reflect on the bus; it would have been equally tedious in a Leyland — well, almost. No, this was one of the long trunk routes beloved of the Scottish Bus Group, that essentially provided a range of short-journey opportunities along its length, but was less used for long trips. Edinburgh-Coatbridge took 1hr 43min, and, er, didn't exactly pass through Scotland's most glorious scenery. The fact that Broxburn and Bathgate were the highlights of the journey may give some of you an idea of what it was like.

The bright spot was Airdrie, and if we had managed to get the front four-across upstairs seat in the lowbridge Regent, I would spend half my journey straining to catch the first glimpse of a Glasgow tram at the Airdrie

Left: Unusual purchases for a Tilling group company were 18 of these 1954 Bedford SBs with Duple 37-seat coach bodies. They were fitted with Gardner 4LK engines. Eastern Counties No BV848 is seen in Norwich bus station.

Left: My 1959 East Anglian Area 'abc' didn't include this bus, so it took a bit of detective work, probably involving reports in Buses Illustrated, to find out that it was one of five prewar Bristol K5Gs acquired by Eastern Counties in 1959 from Bristol Tramways. No LKH27 (FHT 808), fitted with 1949 Bristol-built body, is seen at Norwich Thorpe station.

Right: More modern, but arguably less interesting than the Leyland TD2s, this 1959 Bristol SC4LK with ECW 35-seat bus body is seen in Norwich bus station on the 33A service, complete with typically helpful destination display.

Below right: Parked in the forecourt of the Great Yarmouth Corporation garage is No 14, one of the 1944 Strachan-bodied Guy Arab II. On its right is one of the Weymann-bodied Leyland Titan TD5s.

terminus. This meant not only that we were approaching civilisation — yes, in Airdrie — but that the journey was nearly over. As well as the trams there were unfamiliar SOL buses and the glorious blue buses of Baxter's, one of the most popular independents in Scotland.

Buses Illustrated tended to help with my itineraries. So when I read that Glasgow Corporation had one of the first four production Leyland Atlanteans, I headed west in search of it. And then Laurie of Hamilton bought an Atlantean, and I went in search of that, adding another fascinating fleet to my portfolio. Yes, we really did make pilgrimages to find Atlanteans.

Holiday time

We were lucky that my father always believed in having a real holiday, so each summer we would head off to some boarding house, usually in England. At first it was by the sea, but father became more adventurous and so in the later 1950s we 'did' London, York, East Anglia, Leamington Spa — and Ayr.

A pattern soon emerged. We would breakfast as a family, and while my parents and younger sister went off sightseeing, I would take myself off to the local bus station or, whisper it, railway station, for my earlier interest in trains still persisted. At the end of the day we met up again as a family and I allowed my parents to feed me.

These were good holidays, partly because everything was new. I often knew very little about the local operators, because there weren't always ABCs covering these areas, but that was part of the fun. Other readers will doubtless remember the excitement — and that's not too strong a word for it — of discovering new operators and new

Above: A call at Lincoln returning from our 1960 East Anglia holiday revealed Corporation BVL 398, a 1946 Guy Arab II with Park Royal body, outside the railway station.

Below: At the Boswell Park, Ayr, bus station of AA Motor Services, representatives of the Young's and Dodds fleets. On the left is DAG 388, one of two all-Leyland Titan PD2/1 bought by Young's in 1950; these were the first new double-deckers for Young's AA fleet, which was Leyland-dominated. It was withdrawn in 1965. On the right is Dodds FOP 447, a 1944 Guy Arab II which had been new to Birmingham City Transport with a utility Park Royal body, sold to Dodds in 1950 it received this 1949 ECW body (from a 1933 Hants & Dorset Leyland TD2) the same year. Dodds always favoured Gardner-engined buses.

buses.

Our 1957 London holiday was largely sightseeing, and while the then LT fleet was at its most RT-family-dominated, there was the fun (for me at least) of waiting with my family at Surrey Docks terminus for prototype Routemaster RM1 to arrive on the 260 service. My blind faith that it would arrive was rewarded.

We stayed with relatives at Woodbastwick, near Norwich, in 1957, and although this lovely little village merited a fairly irregular service into Norwich, it did provide such treats as rebodied 1932/33 Leyland Titan TD2s, and a trip on one of these introduced me to the high level of standardisation that could be found in Tilling group companies at this time. Except that Eastern Counties could field some interesting buses as a result of take-overs, and, I suspect, its proximity to Eastern Coach Works. So in addition to the hordes of red-painted Bristols there were ECW-bodied Leyland Titan PD1As, Duple-bodied Bedfords and even Dennis Lancet coaches that had come with the business of Metropolitan of Great Yarmouth.

My fondness for municipal buses took me to Great Yarmouth where this smart little municipality boasted unrebodied 1937/38 Weymann-bodied Leyland TD5s and wooden-seated Guy Arab utilities, as well as my first taste of an open-top double-decker, a 1934 AEC Regent/English Electric. My first ever published photograph was of a Yarmouth TD5, and appeared in *Buses Illustrated* for February 1961.

Ayr travel

My first visit to Ayr, in 1958, was a further revelation. Independent operators were so thin on the ground in Edinburgh as to be almost non-existent, so to 'discover' AA Motor Services was truly educational. The two bus stations in Ayr, AA's and Western SMT's, were within a couple of hundred yards of each other, so it was possible to see a great deal without moving very far. From the box-camera photos I took on that holiday, I seem to have spent much time at AA's Boswell Park station, marvelling at the amazing collection of buses passing through on the long main-road route to Ardrossan, and on the various local services around Ayr.

At that time there were three members of the AA co-operative — Youngs, based at Ayr, Tumilty at Gailes, and Dodds at Troon. Each had its own vehicle policy, and there were the subtle and not-so-subtle livery (and even colour) differences that helped to identify the different owners.

Dodds buses were the easiest. They were usually Guys, virtually everything had Gardner engines, and — a real giveaway this — had 'DT. No.' fleet numbers. Youngs were Leyland fans and favoured a lighter green. Tumilty further helped identification by specialising in Daimlers.

So there was plenty of variety to be seen at Boswell Park. Dodds fielded Guy Arab double-deckers ranging from second-hand utility examples from Birmingham, Glasgow-London and Plymouth, to postwar Park Royal and Roe-bodied examples; there were single-deck Arabs too, postwar buses with Brockhouse and Burlingham bodies, as well as two double-deck chassis rebodied in 1953 with unusual 30ft long Roe centre-entrance bodies. The only non-Guys in the fleet seemed to be an ex-Edinburgh unfrozen Bristol K5G and OKM 317, the former AEC

Top: Two of the more unusual Dodds contributions to the AA fleet are seen at Boswell Park, Ayr. The single-decker is DGG 910, which started life in 1943 as a Glasgow Corporation Guy Arab II double-decker, and when it was bought by Dodds in 1953 the chassis was extended to 30ft long and it received this 38-seat centre-entrance Roe body. Another Guy was similarly treated. They ran in this form until 1965. The double-decker is OKM 317, which was new in 1951 as a demonstrator. It was an AEC Regent III with Saunders-Roe lightweight bodywork owing more than a little to the London RT bodies Saunders had been building. It ran for Dodds from 1953 until 1979, and was withdrawn for preservation.

Above: Resting between trips on a private hire to Leamington Spa in 1959, is a 1949 Coventry Corporation Daimler CVD6 with Brush 34-seat bus body, one of 16 similar vehicles.

Top: Outside the Bird's premises at Stratford-on-Avon in 1959, ex-London Transport RTL269 which may well have seen further service, unlike most of the buses pictured in Tom Moore's article in this book. Unlike Tom, I never ventured further than this.

Above: Sitting in a corner in Stratford-on-Avon in 1959, is this reminder that Stratford Blue was owned by Midland Red. Although the Stratford Blue bus fleet was mainly Leyland, with, surprisingly perhaps, none of Midland Red's own-make BMMO vehicles, there was this 1938 SON type, DHA 731, acting as a tree-lopper.

Regent III demonstrator with RT-like Saunders Roe Rivalloy body; this bus is still preserved by Dodds, along with 1955 Guy Arab IV / Roe GSD 779 and the 1957 Burlingham Seagull-bodied Guy Warrior SJW 515.

Youngs oldest Leyland was a 1942 unfrozen Titan TD7, and it had standard Leyland-bodied PD2 Titans, a Leyland-bodied Royal Tiger, and ex-Yorkshire Woollen Brush-bodied PS1s.

Tumilty's Daimlers included Willowbrook-bodied CVD6 single-deckers, an ex-Viking, Preston CVD6 / Strachans double-decker, an ex-London CWA6, and GAG 970, the magnificent 1954 broad-radiator CD650 model with Northern Counties bodywork.

Although the three fleets apparently had little in common, in 1957 they each received Alexander-bodied double-deckers. Dodds bus was a rebuilt ex-Plymouth Guy Arab II; Young's Leyland was a new PD2 / 20 Titan; and Tumilty's Daimler was a new CVG6.

The fleet details were diligently recorded, and I recall writing to AA with a copy of what I thought was an up-to-date fleetlist asking if they could confirm its accuracy, only to receive a green-typed letter saying that the company 'couldn't see what possible use this information would be.' Ho hum.

Home of the Orion

Leamington Spa in 1959 was quite different. I can't quite remember why we went to Leamington *en famille*, but it was a useful base to enjoy the delights of Warwick and Stratford, and see more of these quaint — to my eyes at least — BMMO designs, including the remnants of the once-large FEDD fleet of forward-entrance double-deckers built in the 1930s. And I had prepared myself sufficiently to make an arrangement to visit the Metropolitan-Cammell factory at Elmdon, whence had come the Orion-bodied Leyland PD2 / 20s that were my daily transport to school by this time. For some reason I didn't take my camera, so my memories are of Manchester Orion PD2s with virtually everything apart from windows painted red, and some early Atlanteans — Maidstone & District green sticks in my mind. I also recall lots of elderly double-deckers that were used for staff transport, standing around the factory, but I didn't think that my hosts would be impressed if this 15-year-old schoolboy rushed off to inspect them rather than the gleaming new buses inside.

Mind you, at least I was probably in long trousers by that time.

Gavin Booth is a freelance writer who has written or edited more than 30 books on buses including Bus Stop and The British Motor Bus. He is editor of Classic Bus magazine.

Left: This former Ribble bodyshop certainly wasn't art deco, and the ex-RAF barrage balloon hangar at Fazackerly, Liverpool, shows another side to the usually spick-and-span image of the company in its heyday. The tenancy of it was secured in March 1948 with the intention of using it for overhauls of South Lancashire allocated vehicles and, at the same time, relieve pressure on Bootle depot, where the desperate need for more accommodation in those hectic postwar years was making life difficult for maintenance staff. It must have been an eerie place, and somewhat inhospitable in winter. The opening of new premises at Aintree in July 1951 made its welcome closure possible, and the relic could then be left alone to the wind, desolation, and, no doubt, ghosts from the dark days of war. This view shows a Duple-rebodied prewar Tiger and a Titan PD1 with Burlingham body sharing the apron with a new Leyland chassis. Peter Hesketh Collection

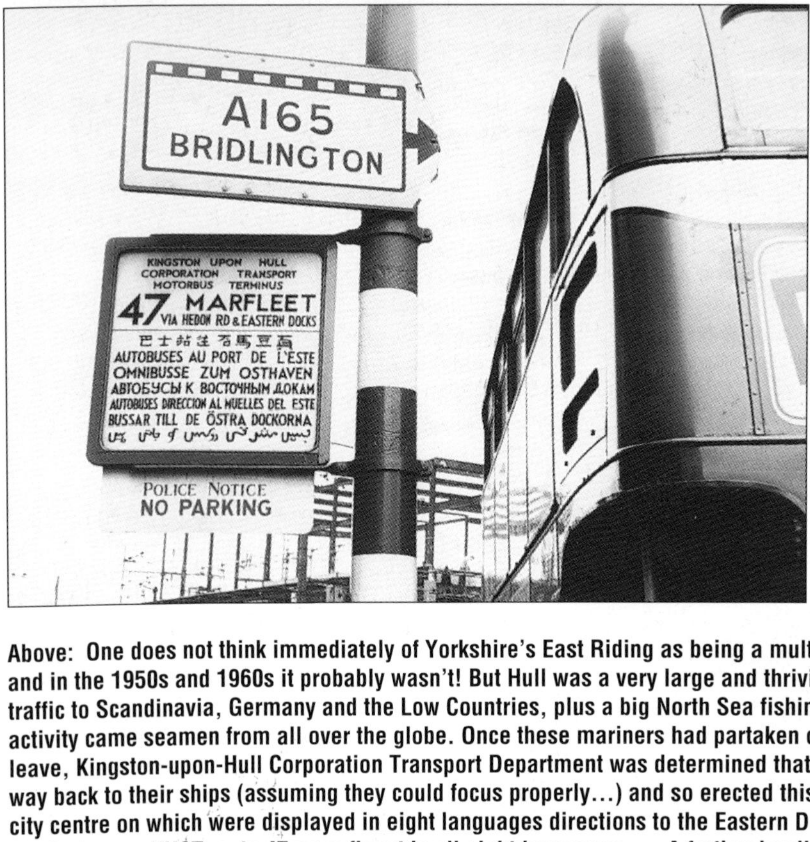

Above: One does not think immediately of Yorkshire's East Riding as being a multi-cultural cosmopolitan area and in the 1950s and 1960s it probably wasn't! But Hull was a very large and thriving seaport with much marine traffic to Scandinavia, Germany and the Low Countries, plus a big North Sea fishing fleet, and with all of this activity came seamen from all over the globe. Once these mariners had partaken of some much-needed shore leave, Kingston-upon-Hull Corporation Transport Department was determined that the 'legless' would find their way back to their ships (assuming they could focus properly...) and so erected this illuminated bus stop in Hull city centre on which were displayed in eight languages directions to the Eastern Docks, and presumably conductors on KHCT route 47 were fluent in all eight languages... . A further implication is that only Brits park illegally. A KHCT AEC Regent III completes this June 1962 scene. Michael Dryhurst

SECOND FIDDLE/2

Above: Winchester bus station. On a site purchased and cleared by Hants & Dorset Motor Services, the bus station was opened on 20 June 1935, the tape being cut by the mayor, Councillor J. O. Hodder, with a pair of gold scissors decorated with an enamelled Hants & Dorset bus. H&D buses had hitherto parked along the pavements of the Broadway along with King Alfred and country buses. The bus station remains active to this day, despite deregulation and the sell-off of Southampton bus station to developers, but the fascia now carries modern lettering and terminology. In this view, taken around 1972, the Royal Green Jackets are seen enjoying their Freedom of the City of Winchester and evidently, despite its being private property, the Freedom of the bus station entrance. H&D Bristols flank an Aldershot & District Dennis Loline; A&D route 14 used the bus station as well. Robert E. Jowitt

Left: The Winchester Bypass was one of the earliest dual carriageways to be built. Opened in the 1930s, its most prominent feature was Spitfire Bridge. With an unusual parabolically-shaped arch, the bridge was named after a World War 2 pilot, believed to be Flt-Lt McGrath of the Royal Canadian Air Force, who flew underneath it. In 1948 a slightly less fast method of transport began to pass underneath the bridge when Venture Ltd introduced a bus service between Basingstoke and Winchester. Competing with a direct rail link and an alternative bus link provided by King Alfred Motor Services, use of the indirect Bypass approach to Winchester was forced on Venture because of objections from established operators on the more direct route via Kingsworthy. The service never prospered and Wilts & Dorset, successors to Venture, eventually abandoned it. Seen here passing beneath Spitfire Bridge on 5 April 1971, two days before final withdrawal, is an empty W&D No 574, an ECW-bodied Bristol LS5G, with a barely useful indicator display that was representative of practice in the area at that time. P. R. Wallis

OF TRAMS AND TEARS AND MATTERS AS IN MIRRORS

ROBERT E. JOWITT, *enfant terrible* of transport literature, tripping to Portugal in the mid 1970s in search of trams and narrow gauge locos, encounters wine (naturally), girls (of course), and an unexpected pleasure in the unlikely local metamorphosis of familiar British buses.

THIS IS not the reason why I am here, this gherkin-coloured spectacle, any more than this brown-eyed olive-skinned nymph is the reason, yet both are marvellous, chance and brief encounters though they be, and could have made a very good reason for coming. The gherkin-coloured spectacle is an AEC halfcab exposed-radiator double-decker and I might think that I was seeing it in a glass darkly for it is completely the wrong way round, only there is no mirror. So I might think I was seeing it in vino; and that could be, though it isn't, the reason for coming here. The reason for coming here is that I dreamed a dream, almost rather a nightmare, in which the glasses of the lamps on the immaculate narrow gauge locomotives were broken or even missing and tears were falling from these damaged eyes. I have to see if such an inconceivable vandalism is true, I have to return to the north of Portugal, and while I'm about it I'm starting off by sampling the trams of Lisboa, a treat I have hitherto denied myself in the firm if mistaken belief that they are immortal. Buses and maidens, whatever their charms, are merely incidental to the intended itinerary.

This is not long after the end of the Salazar era. Unfortunately it is usually necessary to consider public transport in relation to politics. Whatever the evils and repressions of the great Portuguese dictatorship, the effect on tramways is almost

Above: Who needs buses when there are trams not only all around but also above? 1948 Carris Weymann-bodied AEC Regal III No 142 passes under the arch carrying the Rua do Alecrim over the Rua de Santo Paulo. All photographs by Robert E. Jowitt

'sleeping beauty' and until the early 1970s we might be in the 1930s and often earlier with standards of vehicle maintenance to match. Modernity has been sneaking in only with a Metro which you can't see so you can pretend it isn't there, and a fleet of buses which anywhere save Lisboa would be the main reason for visiting the place, but when you can ride every day on trams built in 1906 let alone new ones from the 1920s, 1930s and 1940s, how can you spare any time for the buses?

It's a pity if you can't. If the tram system is largely frozen in the 1930s, the buses are largely

Left: AEC Regal III halfcabs came in three styles. No 123 in the Rua do Arsenal (speeding past what is probably a police station) has three large side windows plus a smaller one ahead of the forward door.

fossilised in the 1950s; a whole fleet of halfcab AECs, double and single-deckers, the chief point of note apart from age being that they are all mirror image. On single-deckers with doors this is nothing too exciting though the halfcab on the wrong side looks odd enough in all conscience, but the open platform on the wrong corner and the steps going up the wrong way, this is really the frogs crawling across the floor after a heavy session in a wine house.

Lisboa abounds in drinking establishments, ranging from fin-de-siécle palaces to sinister sawdust dens, from which you can reach out and almost touch the passing tramcars. Frequently the relationship to the buses is just as close and, it may be argued, more dangerous; the course of the tram is fixed, the course of the bus contains an element of uncertainty.

Maniacal flair

Driving trams in Lisboa is a highly skilled art but driving buses calls for an extra almost maniacal flair. It is hard to do justice in mere words to the experience of riding on one of these AECs. The road surfaces are frequently dreadful, the body of the bus strains in several different directions at every bump, every window leaps in its frame, and you have to hang on for dear life to avoid being thrown to the floor, for the driver considers it essential to drive as fast as he possibly can, with frequent horn play. Only 15 or 20mph seems death-defying when the walls of the houses are about a foot away on either side and the gradients up or down are Alpine. Lisboa boasts of being built on seven hills — and if the trams tackle any gradient they possibly can, plus a few you would imagine they couldn't — they leave the more outrageous to the single deck buses.

The double-deckers behave slightly — only slightly — less dangerously, hurling themselves full tilt, a lot more that 15mph, along the more level avenues through the centre of the city and the wide boulevards beside the Tagus. The windows rattle nearly as much.

One bus on which I ride succeeds by good management (or good fortune and prayer) in meeting oncoming buses only in the broader sections on its headlong career through the alleyways, only to find its passage along the final avenue to the Tagus hindered by a tram; so it overtakes the tram on the wrong side, in the very teeth of an oncoming tram, missing it only by inches… and perhaps further prayer.

Two of the main termini for a great number of buses are on the banks of the Tagus, at the Praça do Comercio, the elegant square designed by the Marquis of Pombal, and the less exalted Cais do Sodre with its market stalls where sun-browned peasants sell wonderful fruit and vegetables. Some of the young girls thus employed are bewitching in their brown-eyed tanned beauty; their mothers are sturdily handsome. The buses tick over and rev up just beyond the stalls. This was not why I came here; the trams are making a constantly changing pattern of yellow only a few yards further away, demanding my attention.

Three types

Still I do become aware that double-deckers appear in three types, and I think single-deckers

Above: No 118 of the small-window type 1948 AEC Regal IIIs bounding along the uncertain surface of the Rua Santa Apolonia at the point where it becomes the Calçada da Cruz da Pedra at the junction with the Calçada dos Barbadhinos (distinguished in the photo by a horse's rump). The typical youths striding so purposefully along are probably heading for a tavern.

come in three's too. In these figures I do not include a newer generation of rear-engine double-deck Daimler Fleetlines or some full-fronted single-deckers of a make I cannot distinguish, and certainly not the future generation of Volvos. The double-deckers with exposed radiators (Regals?) have bodies with forward entrance or with open rear platform while those with Regent-type tin front come only with forward entrance. Single-deck variations are identified by the shape of the front of the roof and the arrangement of doors and windows. Competition from trams (and taverns and brown eyes) makes detailed study of such trifles extremely difficult.

The rarest are the open platforms, probably they are also the oldest so presumably a lot have been scrapped. It can't be too long before all the halfcabs are ousted by the Volvos. With the end of the dictatorship signs of progress are flooding in. Trams are breaking out in horrible all-over advertising, bus and tram crews instead of wearing the formerly renowned smart uniforms are dressing like yobs, and who can blame them when the walls of public buildings are splattered with political posters showing one of the leaders in a scruffy open-neck shirt! He may be a jolly good chap but is this really ministerial material? Dash it all, there are even political posters plastered on the flanks of the buses; this is surely going too far! Come back, Salazar, all is forgiven! Only he's dead, and of course the peasantry will now be richer and less down-trodden, the bright-eyed market girls will trade their rags and naïve charm for the smug anonymous fashions of bourgueosie. Meanwhile what had progress done to the narrow gauge? My nightmare about the locomotive lamps really is the reason why I am here.

Even though it were easy to spend far longer over the halfcabs I am fairly satiated with yellow trams and it's time to head north. Of several diversely awful misadventures which befall me in Portugal the most irritating is, as

Right: AEC Regal III no. 109 descends the narrow alleys from Castelo de São Jorge on route 37. It has a couple of seconds to take the 90° corner round the kerbstone bottom right of picture.

EB-14-30

the Porto train slips out from Lisboa, to discover my sardine tin has no key. I could remedy this by getting out at Coimbra, half way, but I have been there before; I have admired its trams and trolleybuses and even appreciated a fine halfcab Regent there. I have of course been to Porto before too, delighting in its double-deck trolleybuses and a fine fleet of antiquated trams which I know are less immortal than I believe Lisboa's, but to Porto I must go again for the locomotives in the dream were the Porto 0-4-4-0 1906 Henschell Mallets, the most beautiful narrow gauge locomotives ever built.

A collection of bizarre buses is a bonus, when I have time to glance at them, as among their number are more halfcab Regents. The Regents in Coimbra are Lisboa tramway yellow and white, the Regents in Porto

Above: Regal No 130 tackling the gradient of the Calçada da Estrela with a roar and a mighty cloud of exhaust. The citizens are very sensibly not using the sunny side of the street.

Right: The classic Lisboa double-decker is this 1957 Weymann-bodied AEC Regent III with exposed radiator and open rear platform. No 302 at the Praça Marques de Pombal appears to be in trouble. If one way or another the passengers appear unmoved, the intending passengers don't seem put off. From the top of the column the Marques surveys the city he rebuilt after the 1755 earthquake. These were Lisbon's last new exposed-radiator Regents, essentially late-model Regent III although with chassis numbers in the Regent V series.

VARIG
VARIG
SHELL
FOTO
CINE
YASHICA
PIONEIRA EM APARELHOS ELECTRÓNICOS
CARRIS
302

COMICIO
vota
OTELO
COMICIO
vota
OTELO
208
COMICIO
vota
OTELO
COMICIO
vota
OTELO

VELHA
1920

are pale blue and cream. The maids of the Porto markets and the banks of Douro are even more comely than those in Lisboa, and mostly they have the same brown eyes, but one has bewitching green eyes. A smile from those green eyes, though it is not the reason I came here, is some consolation for finding the formerly spotless 0-4-4-0 Mallets now indescribably filthy, some even with that wretched poster pasted on, and nearly all with their lamp glasses cracked or lost completely. This is the reason I have come here, in fear of proving the nightmare, and it has proved too dreadfully true. I surmise I am only just in time to see the Mallets active at all. The only detail not fulfilled is the tears, but I could supply them

Left top: The offside of an 1950 open-platform Weymann-bodied Regent III, No 208, seen passing some restoration work in the Praça do Comercio. This bus has escaped the commercial advertising which disfigures many vehicles, only to be plastered with political posters instead.

Left: Forward-entrance Regals lack the allure of the rear-entrance version but are not devoid of charm. No 462, at the church of Santa Maria in Belem, was built in 1966 and not 1920. The magnificent south door of the church, in the Manueline style, is very early 16th century; the tower is dismissed as a 19th century pastiche. The bus was one of 50 1948 Regals rebodied as 65-seat forward-entrance double-deckers by UTIC in 1966/7.

Above: Whatever the delights of Weymann-bodied Regent V No 353 of 1960, they pale into the insignificance of modernity compared with the almost entirely original perfection of Brill tram No 333 of 1906.

Right: Maria and her mother pictured in the market at Cais do Sodre with an agreeable background of Regent V.

Above: The other sort of single-decker, No 84; Jowitt never found out what these were, merely contented himself with thinking they looked vaguely British. Gavin Booth, however, can tell us that they are Daimler CVU6LXs with UTIC bodies. This is at Cais do Sodre; the statue is of the Duque de Terceira, under whose leadership the liberals defeated the absolutist Don Miguel in 1834. The Daimler CVU was essentially a badge-engineered Guy Victory assembled in Portugal.

Right: The modern generation of double-deckers personified by Carris-bodied Daimler Fleetline No 828 of 1968 in the Praça Dom Pedro IV more generally known as the Rossio, formerly spelt Rocio and usually regarded as the heart of Lisboa. A guide book described the paving (limestone and basalt) as having a curious harmony, but it might prove hazardous for the customers of the several adjacent cafés.

myself for the tragedy of it. Should I not flee, never to return? Half the reason for coming will be gone. Yet for the slightest chance to gain another smile from those beguiling green eyes might not the halfcabs themselves become almost a reason in their own right? I could easily learn to love them very well.

Top: Only the murk of the shop window tells you that the more correct-looking version on the left is in fact the mirror image. No 341 heading up the Rua do Ouro from Comercio is a Regent V of 1958.

Above: Porto profiles. The bus appears to be No 201, the first of 10 1960 AEC Regent V with UTIC bodies.

Above: Coimbra Regent V No 12 advertises port, while passing a lady carrying her goods in the traditional Portuguese fashion.

Robert E. Jowitt was born in Wantage and has spent most of his life in Hampshire, but retreated to Herefordshire in 1989. Like other starving authors he has sometimes perforce been employed as a bar manager, Noddy train driver, etc. He is notorious for his unconventional approach to transport photography as in A Desire of Tramcars, The Girl in the Street, and other publications.

One lump, or two?

A steamy selection from the 'emergency' camera of JOHN G. LIDSTONE

ONE DAY IN 1964, a Southend Corporation Leyland Titan PD2/20 suddenly erupted into a cloud of steam and boiling water at the top of Pier Hill. Instantly realising the potential value of a camera, as a young boy I was determined to be ready to catch any recurrence as soon as my Dad generously obliged. Not one of the tin-fronts obliged ever again — and I soon found that buses don't like being photographed 'on the boil' and usually do so when you can't possibly catch them on film. Undeterred, here are a selection of hot-spots that didn't get away. Such occurrences — 'having the kettle on' — would invariably be talking points back at the depot later on. Or, indeed, at the time — as one vexed Eastern National driver said from the cab of his steaming Bristol FLF: 'one lump or two?'!

Later Bristol Lodekka FLFs with the Cave-Brown-Cave heating and ventilating system could manage a really spectacular 'boil-up.' Superbly simple and often effective, CBC had just one fatal flaw: it wasn't a fully-pressurised system, so as to prevent coolant loss. Main water supply was retained in large radiator tanks at each side of the

Above: Many of Eastern National's LD Lodekkas had Gardner 5LW engines. Here, 'F' is the registration letter, freezing fog the weather. March 1972 at Southend Central station early in the morning and Southend's idling No 2509 merrily boils away to itself while its crew is nowhere to be seen.

Left: Bristol Lodekkas with conventional radiators would also lose control from time to time — even in the cool of March. Standard fare for Eastern National's service 3 in 1974 were 'lazy' semi-automatic Bristol FLF6LXs. An unpopular and audibly tired BVW-engined manual-gearbox No 2711, seen here, would obviously have been happier with its radiator blind lowered, but instead its driver was conspicuously pleased to watch his 'achievement' on this occasion, bringing the likelihood of a changeover for an easier vehicle at nearby Hadleigh depot a mile further on. All photographs by John G. Lidstone

Above: A memorable encounter on 15 March 1977 was Eastern National's No 2888 en route from the well-known Wood Green, London 'On the buses' depot to Southend on marathon service 251. Having already boiled-over several times on its London-bound journey, the photographer encountered it being replenished at London Transport's Romford garage, photographed it boiling over at Hutton, and a few miles further on, the driver decided to replenish his recalcitrant beast yet again. No sooner had he jumped out of the cab, than the radiator cap burst open, such was the accumulated pressure. Driver Healey scampers away from the Vesuvian eruption taking place behind him.

Left: White out! No 2888, again, billows steam from every orifice. Normal service was resumed as soon as possible — a while later. Handy-can came to the rescue once more!

indicator blinds, in the upper saloon. Located behind thermostatically-controlled shutters, these tanks were without any kind of fan to cool them — should the shutters stick, boiling point would be quickly reached, which is why many could be seen with small blocks of wood wedged in between the vanes to keep them open. Reliant solely upon the natural airflow for cooling, slow-moving traffic (or even a following wind) could soon cause overheating if circumstances conspired. Pressure

Top: The larger Gardner 6LX engine of the FLF6LX seemed to tax the CBC system more than it could deliver in sultry shining sun or with trailing wind. A hot 29 June 1977 sees Eastern National's No 2915 from Wood Green depot spewing precious coolant in the few minutes at rest in Southend prior to its marathon return journey to London just a few minutes later. Amazingly, the Gardner engines could withstand prolonged cooking in this manner; seizures were rare.

Middle: Boiling exposed-radiator Leylands were a very uncommon sight, at least in Southend. Here No 341 has just returned to traffic after a period off the road, and all is not well. A soft rear tyre, scroll-winding gear falling to pieces, and a leaky radiator drain valve all conspired to terminate this journey at Eastern National's Hadleigh depot, thereby making a change from the constant stream of boiling Bristol FLFs calling there for rescue. The PD3 smoulders while the photographer-driver goes in search of the watering-can on 15 December 1977.

Bottom: Southend Corporation's chief inspector was well known for his ability to appear suddenly as if from nowhere. In this case he suddenly emerged from a nearby hedge(!) and, spotting steam, he duly summoned a labourer from an adjacent building site to top up No 341 from a muddy puddle using a bucket and funnel, leaves and all, despite the driver's protestations!

Left: A radiator leak has brought Guernsey Motors' 1958 Albion Victor FT39KAN/Reading No 76 to the boil *en route* for St Peter Port. A cloud of steam billows round the cab to the surprise of the passing motorbiker in June 1978.

Below left: A long journey from sunny Worthing on the south coast to a baking hot Epsom for The Derby on 7 June 1978 has caused a problem for thirsty Southdown Bristol BVW-engined FS6B, No 2503, almost out of water. Swerving off the main road at speed to park on the racecourse, it merrily billows steam from its bonnet vent. Its jolly upper-saloon punter-passengers are already too carefree to notice that their grandstand is boiling; the grim-faced driver had obviously had his fill already, however.

would then force out most of the contents of the boiling system through the narrow-diameter overflow vent pipe just in front of the bonnet lid, behind the cowl. Using this handy spout, well-trained Eastern National specimens could aim and fire a jet of boiling water right up the front of the bus and occasionally right into the push-out ventilators of the upper saloon. At this point the vehicle would normally be laid to rest at the kerbside to cool down.

The sudden appearance of this steaming geyser was quite a novel experience for the upper deck front-seat passengers, whilst passers-by would witness brown water cascading down all over the place — in winter accompanied by huge swirling clouds of steam. Great stuff for the camera (but not for the unwary conductor caught napping). Once the brief fountain display was over, ever-increasing clouds of steam would then issue from the same point, in winter creating a superb display, with wafting white steam clouds trailing the whole length of the vehicle at speed, or billowing over the roof when stationary.

Left: Battle-scarred Southend open-top Leyland PD3, PHJ 951, takes a break at the Kursaal — the cream paintwork on its front bulkhead rapidly turning brown as a result of a failing head-gasket.

Below left: A cool and wet 21 April 1978 does not deter Bexleyheath's RT4566 from a lively boil-up. A roaring jet of steam blasts the road as the RT continues, picking up its passengers.

Below: When RM1543 was purchased by Southend Transport, nobody thought to check that the radiator contained the appropriate antifreeze mix. A sudden cold snap on its second day in service duly froze the unblanked radiator, with the result that most of its water had been blown out over the nearside wing in the slow-moving traffic caused by the bitterly cold (26°F) conditions. The duty crew came to the rescue and Southend No 116 was despatched home to recover. It reappeared in the even colder (22°F) evening peak, duly replenished with antifreeze mix, without any problems at all.

HOLIDAY BUSES AND COACHES

Summer holiday journeys to the seaside evoke happy memories for PAUL KELLY

MY PARENTS were creatures of habit so far as holidays were concerned. Having exhausted Colwyn Bay and Old Colwyn as a holiday destination for most of the 1950s they turned their attention from the North Wales coast to the West Country for our 1959 family holiday which was to Burnham-on-Sea in North Somerset.

Coach travel was always preferred to rail, so on a Saturday morning in late August we found ourselves in the queue at the Pembroke Place/Collingwood Street terminus in Liverpool which served as the departure point for Ribble's express services, those for Cheltenham, for connecting services to the West Country, and elsewhere, being numbered X24.

In common with other operators of express services, Ribble hired in vehicles from other operators on busy summer Saturdays in order to cope with demand. Thus our coach to Cheltenham was a most surprising vehicle being a Foden PVRF6 with early Plaxton Panorama bodywork finished in the maroon and turquoise livery of Toppings, a small Liverpool coach operator. It was new in 1959 and registered 367 CKA. I believe this was the last Foden psv built for the home market before the unsuccessful Foden-NC double-decker of the mid-1970s.

Toppings had a mixed coach fleet at the time and I remember seeing a Harrington-bodied Bedford SB of 1960 and a Plaxton-bodied Bedford VAL of 1964, both bought new, being used on hire to Ribble during the 1960s. Another local coach operator used by Ribble was Hardings of Birkenhead which maintained a smart fleet of mainly Plaxton-bodied AEC Reliances, also bought new, which were distinctive for having registration numbers in round hundreds eg PCM 600. I rode on one such coach to Scarborough in 1966 but that belongs to another story.

On arrival at St Margaret's coach station in Cheltenham, there was an appetising array of coaches, seemingly from all over the country, for the young bus enthusiast to drool over. Apart from the AEC Reliances, Bristol Ls, Guy Arab LUFs and Leyland Royal Tigers of Black & White Motorways, all with exotic-looking bodywork, there were the equally unusual Albions, Guys and Leylands of Red

Above: The rear-engined Foden PVRF6 with Plaxton Panorama bodywork, 367 CKA, new in 1959 to Toppings, Liverpool, is seen in August 1959 at the Raven Hotel, Prees Heath, Shropshire-operating on hire to Ribble on the latter's X24 Liverpool-Cheltenham service.
P. J. Kelly

& White with destinations painted in white on the nearside front window, like a greengrocer's shop! All of these were unusual to me at the time because I was yet to discover *Buses Illustrated* or the various Ian Allan ABC fleet books which, within a few years, were to be responsible for keeping me in touch with the bus world at large. Coaches running south and west of Cheltenham were often 'On hire to Associated Motorways' as was our conveyance to Weston-Super-Mare, a halfcab coach either of Baker's of Weston or WEMS. In later years both were to be familiar names in the provision of extra coaches 'on hire' on summer Saturdays.

Leyland zoo

On arrival at Weston, the last part of our long journey to Burnham-on-Sea was completed on a Western National Bristol L service bus. From 1960 Paignton was the family holiday destination and for the next few years or so Ribble provided its own coaches for all the outward and return journeys which I can remember. These were all members of the Leyland 'zoo', Royal Tigers, Tiger Cubs and Leopards. In 1951 Ribble had purchased 120 Royal Tiger PSU1/15s with Leyland coach bodies followed by a further 25 in 1953 and these

Top: Typical of the Ribble coaches in use on the X24 service in the early 1960s was No 858, a Leyland Royal Tiger PSU1/15, one of 130 with centre-entrance Leyland coach bodies delivered in 1951. It is seen arriving at St Margaret's coach station, Cheltenham, in the early 1960s.
D. C. Mitchell collection

Above: At the refreshment stop at the Western National depot and bus station at Taunton on 2 September 1959, this Daimler CVD6 of Wessex Coaches, Bristol, is bound for Exeter on hire to Associated Motorways. The 35-seat Plaxton bodywork was new in 1952, but the chassis, new to Harkness, Penrith, dates from around 1946.

Left: Road and rail run parallel to the sea at Dawlish where Devon General No DRD762, a 1956 AEC Regent V MD3RV with Metro-Cammell 59-seat bodywork, pauses at the stop which was also the picking-up and setting-down point for express services, *en route* to Torquay on 3 September 1959.
K. W. Swallow

Above: As well as operating a substantial number of coaches in Royal Blue livery, Western National had coaches with its own fleetname in a cream and green livery. One example is No 1302, a 1951 Bristol LL6B with Duple coachwork, seen at Dartmouth in June 1956, though still a familiar sight in the early 1960s.
K. W. Swallow

Left: On the same day at the Greenslades Tours booking office in Dawlish, this Greenslades AEC Regal III 9621A with Duple 32-seat bodywork awaits departure on one of the many day-excursions advertised on the boards on the pavement. This classic coach was new in 1950 to the Devon General Grey Cars fleet and was sold to Greenslades in 1958.
K. W. Swallow

Above: Western and Southern National specified this style of ECW coach body with roof-mounted luggage rack for its first batches of Bristol LS6Bs for the Royal Blue fleet. Dating from 1952, No 1292 was seen at London's Victoria coach station.
S. J. Kelly collection

36 SANDYGATE
DAY-HALF DAY AND EVENING TOURS
See the West Country by
GREY CARS
COACHES
FOR PRIVATE HIRE
DEVON GENERAL
DEVON GENERAL
DUO 322

ON HIRE TO ROYAL BLUE
GREY CARS
962 HTT
LONDON
934 GTA

formed the backbone of the express service fleet for a decade or more. In 1960 they still seemed to be in front-line service on the longer routes despite the arrival of later batches of Royal Tigers and Tiger Cubs with Burlingham Seagull bodies, the all-time classic 1950s coach design. The seating layout on centre-entrance coaches, like the 41-seat Leyland-bodied Royal Tigers offered the fortunate passenger a seat on the nearside front, alongside the driver. Unfortunately I was always beaten to it by other passengers. Instead I was usually cocooned somewhere in the middle near the hatch which gave access to the underfloor O.600 engine and although well sound-proofed, tended to give off exhaust fumes.

The journey south from Liverpool to Paignton took all day in pre-motorway days; leaving the city via Bowring Park, Huyton and Prescot then on to Warrington and the north Shropshire town of Whitchurch. As well as being the northwestern-most point of Midland Red territory and the most southerly of Crosville's English operations, Whitchurch was the home of Salopia Saloon Coaches whose two-tone green Duple-bodied Bedfords could be seen at the first refreshment stop, Prees Heath. The cafe here and the adjoining Raven Hotel seemed to have changed little over the years, still being used as a refreshment stop for summer excursion coaches heading north from the West Midlands to North Wales. The coaches of numerous Midlands independent operators together with Fords of Central Coachways, Walsall and various Midland Red coaches, would stop at Prees Heath and it was also common to see one of the aforementioned Salopia Bedfords working a local stage service. Midland Red would be encountered for most of the rest of the journey because of the extensive express services, particularly between Birmingham and Torbay. Although there would be many of Midland Red's

Above left: Devon General DR710, one of the AEC 'light six' rebuilds with 0662 chassis numbers and Weymann Orion 58-seat bodies, is caught at Newton Abbot on 24 May 1960. These buses were all withdrawn in 1963. K. W. Swallow

Left: Grey Cars would often provide duplicates for Royal Blue services at peak times. Waiting at Paignton bus station before departing for London are Nos 962 and 934, a pair of AEC Reliance 2MU3RVs with Willowbrook Viscount 7ft 6in wide 41-seat bodies dating from 1962 and 1961 respectively.
S. J. Kelly

own-make single-deck buses, dual purpose vehicles and coaches (more accurately described as BMMO) by the mid-1960s, Leyland Leopards with early style of BET Federation 36ft long dual-purpose bodywork, would often be used on the summer Saturday express service.

From Prees Heath the Ribble route would proceed through Shropshire via Wellington, Dawley and Bridgnorth, where I might have caught a glimpse of a Wolverhampton Corporation single-decker on the route between the two towns. South of Bridgnorth on the A442 to Kidderminster the first of many Duple-bodied Bedfords of Whittle of Highley would be seen. This operator, as well as running a network of local stage services in the area, also ran its own express services to the Torbay area. From Kidderminster the route would continue via Worcester and Tewkesbury to Cheltenham but duplicate through coaches from Liverpool to Paignton bypassed Cheltenham altogether and took a refreshment stop elsewhere, though exactly where I can't remember. We were now in Bristol Omnibus territory and as, by this date, most of the buses of the associated Cheltenham & District Traction Company that I can remember were of the Bristol/ECW combination, this was to be the diet of the main local bus operators until we reached Exeter. The red and cream livery of the Cheltenham company provided some relief from the Tilling green and cream. All the Bristol Omnibus group buses had a different style of destination layout to most of the rest of the Tilling Group operators which also made them seem very 'different.'

These were, however, still very much the formative years of my education as a bus enthusiast. My only reference books were the Ian Allan ABCs for Ribble and Lancashire Municipals so it is little wonder that I couldn't understand why Bristol Omnibus and Western National buses looked the same as the much more familiar Crosville! The route continued to Bristol, skirting the city centre and passing beneath the Clifton suspension bridge.

Ornate embellishments

By now it would be mid-afternoon and there would be many coaches to be seen, some travelling to and from various West Country destinations and Cheltenham. Even though the spa town itself had probably been bypassed there would still be plenty of Black & White coaches to be seen including AEC Reliances, Guy Arab LUFs,

Above: Departing from Newton Abbot bus station at 10.50am on 24 May 1960 on Devon general's service 12 to Brixham, new Roe 75-seat bodied Leyland Atlantean PDR1/1 No DL912 passes Weymann-bodied AEC Reliance SR797 on layover. Note the shallower roof line on the Roe body compared with the equivalent MCW product.
K. W. Swallow

Leyland Leopards and Royal Tigers with a mixture of Duple, Plaxton and Willowbrook bodywork. The older examples were particularly noted for their ornate embellishments and white wheel-nut covers and all were usually in immaculate condition. By comparison the Duple-bodied Bedfords of Wessex Coaches, Bristol were rather mundane, the 'Queen Mary' style ECW-bodied Bristol LWLs of Bristol Greyhound, complete with greyhound logo, rather less so.

Beyond Bristol the route passed a bus depot at Highbridge in Somerset which was home to some of the Tilling green buses mentioned above. As Highbridge was one of those border towns between two area agreement operators, in this case Bristol Omnibuses and Western National, the depot may have been shared. Our 1959 holiday at nearby Burnham-on-Sea had seen our family use the stage services of both operators to get about on our day trips. The final refreshment stop was at Taunton, firmly in Western National territory at the time and Ribble used the facilities of the Western National bus station and depot for its passengers. There would be several examples of the Western fleet of Bristol/ECW buses to be seen here, including the comparatively rare Albion-engined SUL4A which Crosville did not have!

The city of Exeter was usually by-passed though;the A38 trunk road was usually heavily congested on Saturdays in pre-motorway days, leading to considerable delays before we reached our final destination. As well as the first glimpses of the dark red and cream Devon General buses it was usually also possible to see the odd Exeter Corporation vehicle on the Exeter by-pass or elsewhere in the outskirts of the city, particularly if the Ribble driver had been forced to take a detour to avoid further congestion. There are no particular Exeter vehicle types I recall, though a Massey-bodied Guy Arab or Leyland Titan PD2 would be likely.

The first setting-down point for southbound passengers which I can recall was at Dawlish where both here and at neighbouring Teignmouth, road, railway and sea were in parallel, so the alighting passengers were literally at the seaside as soon as they stepped off the coach. It is likely, however, that only the service coach called at Dawlish and Teignmouth and that if we were travelling on one of the duplicate vehicles we would proceed straight to Torquay to drop the first passengers, sometimes only leaving a handful of us on board for Paignton. In the early 1960s, express services would terminate in a large open car park off the sea front, which offered few facilities for passengers waiting to board for the return journey.

I will always associate this occasionally windswept coach-park at Paignton with the Harrington Cavalier body which could be seen there on Leyland Leopards and AEC Reliances of Southdown, Yelloway and Grey-Green, an

Above: A busy scene on Paignton seafront in the early 1960s sees Devon General 'Sea Dog' class Leyland Atlantean PDR1/1 No 930 *Sir Thomas Howard* loading for Brixham while MCW-bodied stablemate *Sir John Hawkins* heads in the opposite direction. Both were new in 1961 and gave many years' service. The divided opening windscreen was an unusual feature on an Atlantean. S. J. Kelly collection

operator I encountered for the first time at Paignton. I also saw my first 36ft long coach there, a Black & White Leopard with the early style of Plaxton Panorama body for 36-footers, featuring the split rear window. The previously mentioned Midland Red Leopards with dual-purpose bodywork and split windscreens of the early BET design for 36-footers would also be seen here along with BMMO's own-design C5 coaches, which always looked immaculate.

Night journeys

After the frustration of the traffic delays on the then notorious Exeter bypass, mum and dad latched on to the idea of travelling from Liverpool to Devon by night. Ribble operated peak summer season departures from Liverpool on Friday evenings, leaving at about 8pm. The route was the same as already described and I clearly remember the coach calling at the Midland Red depot in Charlton Street, Wellington to pick up passengers at what seemed to me at the time to be an ungodly hour but was probably no later than about 10.30pm. Over 30 years later this location was to be a few minutes walk from the office I occupied from December 1987 to June 1993. During part of that time Charlton Street, by now owned by the British Bus subsidiary, Midland Red North, also housed several ex-Ribble Leyland Leopard/Duple coaches of 1980 vintage, albeit downgraded to dual-purpose vehicles. This overnight service also called at Cheltenham for a refreshment stop though we were probably travelling in the service coach because I also remember stopping somewhere else in the south Midlands, having bypassed Cheltenham altogether.

By the time we reached Taunton, the more sensible people at the Western National depot, having enjoyed a good night's sleep in their beds, were just beginning to emerge from their slumbers to face another busy summer Saturday. You will gather that as far as I was concerned overnight travel by coach was not popular, because to this day I can only sleep in bed at night. Furthermore it was well nigh impossible to see, let alone identify any other buses or coaches the junior bus enthusiast might wish to see in the dark, not to mention not being able to see the passing countryside. Give me day-time travel and traffic jams anytime.

Nevertheless the rest of the family seemed to arrive at their holiday destination enthusing about

Above: The author returned from Paignton to Liverpool in 1962 on a Ribble Leyland Leopard L2 with Harrington Cavalier 41-seat coachwork. No 1025 is seen when new at Skelhorn Street coach station, Liverpool. This vehicle was one of eight from this batch later down-seated to 32-seat tour coaches.
S. J. Kelly collection

all the traffic jams they'd missed and gaining an extra day's holiday while I looked and felt like a zombie!

If there was a highlight to overnight travel it was the arrangement Ribble must have had with a fellow BET operator, Devon General, to refuel its coaches at the latter's Newton Road, Torquay depot ready for the return journey to Liverpool. So it was about breakfast time the coach would pull into the refuelling bay past rows of smart AEC Regents, Reliances and the odd Commer, Leyland or Albion Nimbus, not to mention numerous Atlanteans, all in their dark red and white livery. Perhaps most intriguing of all though were the cream demountable roofs stored on mobile racks inside the depot. These were of course from the famous Sea Dog class Leyland Atlanteans numbered DL925-933 and all named after famous seafarers with Devonian connections. I remember these when they were only a few months old in July 1961 and without doubt the Sea Dogs were my favourite Atlanteans proudly carrying their names, comprehensive destination blinds and additional destination boards beneath the lower deck windows.

The open-top Atlanteans operated on three routes, all starting at Babbacombe and travelling via Torquay and Paignton seafronts to Broadsands, Kingswear or Brixham, numbered 12A, 12C and 12D respectively. These routes were themselves variations of the 'mainline' 12 service from Newton Abbot to Brixham which must have been one of Devon General's busiest routes during the summer months.

Raucous exhaust

After we had safely arrived at our holiday accomm-odation on the outskirts of Paignton, there was plenty to interest the young bus enthusiast. Although our holiday 'digs' were within walking distance of the beach at the Preston end of Paignton seafront, if we chose to take the bus it would be a Regent III operating the 104/105 service from the bus station to Foxhole Estate. After we alighted, the bus began a steep climb towards its destination, accompanied by a raucous exhaust note.

Paignton bus station had been rebuilt in 1960/61 and there was always plenty to see. Leyland Atlantean PDR1/1s with MCW or Roe bodies from the three batches delivered in 1959, 1960 and 1961 were the mainstay of many of the Torbay area services by the early 1960s but there were still plenty of attractive AEC Regent IIIs, mainly from the MTT and NTT registered batches of 1951/52, all with Weymann bodies; the occasional Leyland Royal Tiger from a batch of five with Willowbrook bodies dating also from 1951 and lowbridge Titan PD2/1s of similar vintage. Then there were the rather curious little Albion Nimbus, six from 1958 with Willowbrook bodies and three from 1963 with Harrington bodies, all B31F. Arguably more curious and certainly more interesting to the enthusiast were the 20 'Light Sixes', rebuilt AEC Regents containing a mixture of prewar Regent and Regal parts from a variety of sources and fitted with new Weymann H33/26R bodies except for the first, which was by Saunders Roe. Devon General's Grey Cars coach fleet consisted mainly of AEC Reliances plus a dozen Commer Beadle TS3s with Beadle C41F bodies. Most of the Reliances had Willowbrook bodywork and all coaches were only 7ft 6in wide to enable them to negotiate narrow West Country lanes. The only exceptions were two coaches used on long-distance tours which were built to the more usual 8ft width and these had Weymann Fanfare bodies, new in 1955. From 1964 Harrington Grenadier bodywork was chosen. Livery was grey and maroon with the fleetname on a bar and roundel, similar to LT. We took a day excursion on one of the latter to Newquay in 1964.

The Grey Cars fleet always appeared smartly turned out, adding to the air of romanticism sometimes associated with holiday coach operators. The same was also true of the Royal Blue fleet which had one of the best of all the pre-NBC coach liveries. The various Bristol types used by both the Southern and Western National fleet on Royal Blue express services were a familiar sight in Paignton as they passed through on the Plymouth to London service. The roof-mounted luggage rack, reached by a ladder attached to the rear panelling, was a feature more associated with the 1930s but could still be seen on the last of the Duple-bodied LL6Bs and the earliest of the ECW-bodied LS6Bs. There were also numerous Bristol MWs and the first of the RELH6Gs were beginning to appear in 1964. The Western and Southern National companies also had coaches in their respective fleets which wore a cream and green livery and could be found not only on excursion duties but also frequently on hire to Royal Blue. I remember the batch numbered 1385-1397 (254-266 KTA) when they were new in 1962.

Four-abreast seating

Western National also operated a small number of stage services in the Torbay area, one of which ran from Exeter to Plymouth via Torquay and Paignton, using mainly Bristol Lodekkas of various types. Another, using lowbridge Bristol Ks, ran from Paignton bus station to the village of Stoke Gabriel, a popular destination for holiday-makers. I remember cramming into the typical Tilling-style four-abreast seating on the top deck one warm evening for the well-loaded trip.

When about eight or nine years old most of the Grey Cars coaches passed to fellow BET operator, Greenslades Tours, based in Exeter whose coaches in their mustard and green livery were also a familiar sight in Paignton. Excursions and private hires were operated but again there was much activity in the Associated Motorways and Royal Blue express networks. Greenslades also bought new coaches, AEC Reliances and Bedfords of various types with bodywork by Duple and Harrington. Devon General and Greenslades were not alone in specifying 7ft 6in wide coaches to meet the special Devon operating conditions. The Leeds-based Wallace Arnold concern maintained a small fleet of coaches based in Torquay, built to these dimensions and these too could be seen satisfying the seemingly insatiable demands of holiday-makers to see the Devon countryside from the comfort of a coach. Leyland Leopards and AEC Reliances were the choice, all bought new, with Wallace Arnold remaining loyal to its Yorkshire roots by specifying Plaxton bodywork. I once had a commercial postcard of one of Wallace Arnold's Reliances with early style of Plaxton Panorama bodywork, negotiating a narrow bridge on Dartmoor. Significantly, despite all the upheaval affecting all the operators mentioned so far in this account, Wallace Arnold is one of the few whose public image remains virtually unchanged to this day.

The return journey to Liverpool would always be on one of Ribble's own coaches providing a through service. Thankfully we always travelled home by day, despite encountering those same traffic jams. One or two of these may have been on one of the Burlingham Seagull-bodied Tiger Cubs of which there were 73 delivered between 1954 and 1958. In 1961 there were 12 Leopard L2s with Harrington Cavalier C41F bodies for express duties and one of these took us home in 1962 and the following year the first 36ft long coaches, a batch of 20 with Harrington Cavalier C49F bodies on Leopard PSU3/3R chassis, were the order of the day for the Paignton service. A further 21, with Plaxton Panorama bodies in 1964 significantly modernised the Ribble coach fleet in the four years since our first journey from Liverpool to Paignton.

Paul Kelly was born and brought up in Liverpool and his father worked for Liverpool Corporation Passenger Transport on both trams and buses. Paul has a lifelong interest in buses and is former chair and current member of the Merseyside Bus Club.

Classic Bus Alphabet/4

U IS FOR UNITED. A nice feeling of togetherness. Add the word 'United' to your bus company, and it's reassuring. United Automobile, United Counties, United Welsh, United Bus. Only thing is — United Welsh, once a thriving bus operator now only survives as the coaching arm of Badgerline fleet, Brewers, and United Bus, a brave attempt to unite smaller bus manufacturers in the late 1980s, turned out to be less than the sum of its parts and lasted only four years. United is an anagram of untied.

V IS FOR VANGUARD, a London operator without whom there might well have been no AEC and at least one chunk of Classic Bus readers would have been denied their favourite bus marque. Vanguard didn't buy AECs, but its maintenance workshops in Walthamstow were turned into a bus factory after Vanguard merged with the London General Omnibus Co in 1908. The Associated Equipment Co was formed in 1912 and the rest is history. Right up until it closed in 1979, AEC's Southall works had the telegraphic address 'Vangastow' for 'Vanguard' and 'Walthamstow'.

W IS FOR WEIGHT. It's always been a concern both of operators and manufacturers. By keeping unladen weights down, manufacturers were able to offer operators the potential to squeeze more passengers in within the legally-defined gross vehicle weight.

On two-axle double-deckers in the late 1930s this became a matter of growing concern and Coventry Corporation was one of the leaders in the field, with low-weight Daimlers.

After the war, as weight limits were slowly relaxed, the concern became one of operating economy. Carting unnecessary weight around added to fuel bills. Thus were born a generation of lighter weight single-deckers, the Reliance.

But perhaps the most (in)famous of lightweights were Edinburgh Corporation's mid-1950s Titans with MCW Orion bodies which, thanks to a very spartan interior trim, weighed only 6.6 tons — which was around a ton less than most other operators' double-deckers of the time.

X IS FOR X. Well, that's fairly obvious really. But as the Classic Bus dictionary has only Xanthippe ('shrewish wife'), xebec (a three-masted Mediterranean ship), xenon (a heavy inert gas), xenophobia (morbid dislike of foreigners, which at a pinch could be applied to Leyland when the Metro Scania first appeared), xylonite (celluloid) and xylophone under X, what else can one say? Unless one talks about the Stalybridge, Hyde, Mossley & Dukinfield Joint Transport & Electricity Board Massed Xylophone Band, which we don't intend to, not least because there probably wasn't one.

Right: Xenophobia struck British manufacturers when the Anglo-Swedish Metro-Scania hit the streets in 1970. This was an early Leicester Corporation example. A. P. Newland

X is something you stick in front of a route number, if you want to impress everybody by suggesting that this is the fastest, most dynamic means of getting from A to B, or stick after the number if you're in Manchester, to mean, well, just about anything you want it to mean. It was really short for 'extra' in the latter context, as opposed to 'express' in the former, except that in Manchester it was used much more liberally than that. In the days when there weren't more operators than passengers in Manchester there was a great deal of need for duplication in the peak hours — Manchester had even sharper peaks than most other centres of bus operation. But there were some services which were timetabled as Xs, involving a short-working or deviation from the normal route. There was even a 0x, which seemed to be some works journey to do with Trafford Park. So the numeral blinds on Manchester buses didn't just go from 0 to 9, but went 0, 0x, 1, 1x, 2, 2x etc etc. As a result drivers couldn't always be bothered turning it all the way to the correct number, and often stopped at the x-version. It gave rise to the well-known Manchester bus driving expression, 'xxxx this for a game of soldiers', which meant 'I can't be bothered turning this xxxx handle any further', so the bus which came in as, say, a 54, went out as a 53x rather than a 53, not as any short working, extra or anything else. And no-one seemed to mind too much, because it was almost xpected. The likes of Ribble and North Western ran all sorts of X-numbered express services out of Manchester too, including the most famous of the lot, the X60 to Blackpool, which was at one time the most intensive express service anywhere in the world.

Y IS FOR YORKSHIRE, always good bus territory, where it seemed to be important to get 'Yorkshire' in your company name. So you have, or had, Y Rider, Y Traction, Y Woollen, East Y, South Y (two of them), West Y (two of them), and Y Terrier, not to mention South Riding and West Riding. So why did Lancashire only have East Lancashire Coachbuilders, Lancashire United and South Lancashire? (Well, I suppose there was Selnec — see 'E' — but that's not the point). And wasn't York-West Yorkshire pushing things a bit?

Above: Low-floor buses? We'll have nowt o' that in Yorkshire! If a high-floor AEC Reliance with Park Royal body was good enough for Yorkshire Woollen in 1959, then it was good enough for us.

Z IS FOR ZEUS. Well, you try and come up with anything better. Zeus was Gilford's most successful double-decker, but if you know your Gilfords you'll realise that's a pretty empty claim. Launched in 1932, the year after its revolutionary front-wheel-drive 'decker failed to take the market by storm, this conventionally-designed rival for that other Greek god, the Leyland Titan, clocked up two or maybe three sales. Gilford was the short-lived king of the coach market in the early 1930s, but went under soon after most of its customers were compulsorily acquired by LT . The Zeus might as well have been the Zero.

VENTURERS TO VIKINGS

STEWART J. BROWN tells the story of postwar Albions for Scottish customers.

TODAY there's only one truck and bus builder in Scotland. The company is Volvo. It's Swedish. And it's based in Irvine. Fifty years ago there was also only one truck and bus builder in Scotland. Then the company was Albion. It was Scottish. And it was based in Scotstoun, on the west side of Glasgow.

The postwar boom saw Albion building trucks and buses for operators at home and abroad. Albion double-deckers could be found in far-flung places — such as South Africa and Australia — and the company's rugged single-deckers were a popular choice in British colonies where rough roads and rudimentary workshops really put its products to the test. And it was a test which they generally passed with flying colours, as repeat orders showed.

But what was happening back home in Scotland? Glasgow Corporation Transport, with a fleet of around 900 buses and 1,200 trams at the end of the war, was about to embark on a fairly major programme of fleet renewal.

The bulk of early postwar orders went to AEC and Daimler. Both makers offered buses with preselector gearboxes, a feature to ease the driver's task, in busy cobbled streets with slow-moving traffic, already a problem at peak periods all these years ago. Albion offered a crash gearbox. Delightful on the ear, but hard on the driver.

Left: Glasgow Corporation remained faithful to the Albion Venturer double-decker. This CX19, seen heading back to Parkhead garage in the mid-1950s, was one of nine 1948 examples with rather upright Roberts bodywork. Stewart J. Brown Collection

Right: Another Glasgow Venturer, a 1950 CX37S, is No B107 fitted with rather more stylish Brockhouse bodywork. It lasted in Glasgow service until 1963. This was a real Clydeside product — Brockhouse bodies were built at Clydebank using Park Royal frames. Stewart J. Brown Collection

Glasgow in the end ordered a respectable 138 Venturers from Albion. The first 48 were CX19s with Albion's 105bhp 9.1-litre engine; the final 90 were more powerful CX37s with 9.9-litre engines rated at 120bhp.

Heroic performers

They were bodied by a profusion of long-forgotten builders — Roberts, Metro-Cammell, Brockhouse, Scottish Aviation, Croft and Weymann — and despite having manual gearboxes gave the city on average some 11 years service. By comparison contemporary AECs and Daimlers lasted 14 years. The Albions were latterly concentrated at Parkhead garage in the east, and performing heroically and noisily on the steep hills leading to Castlemilk and Croftfoot on the city's southern edge.

The last was taken out of service in 1963. One survives in Glasgow's first-rate transport museum.

One other Albion found its way into the Glasgow fleet. This was an underfloor-engined single-decker, the KP71. It entered service in 1952, by which time underfloor engines were becoming reasonably widespread — but what made the KP71 interesting was that it had a horizontally-opposed eight-cylinder engine. Fitted with a dual-door Scottish Aviation body, the KP71 was doomed almost from the start. Albion had been taken over by Leyland in 1951 and Leyland's Royal Tiger was doing very well thank you, without competition from the KP71. Not, it has to be said, that the KP71 would have provided much competition. Albion's great days as a bus builder were over.

The only other Scottish operator to put a fleet of Venturers into service after World War 2 was Western SMT. It took 16, all CX37s with lowbridge Alexander bodywork. Western SMT wasn't concerned about the absence of a fluid transmission. Indeed, like most SMT companies it did its best to avoid that particular complication. But the fleet was predominantly Leyland, and was to remain that way for some years to come. The Venturers lasted 12 years with Western; contemporary Leyland Titans averaged 15 years and some even ran for 20.

Western, incidentally, operated the only other KP71 to be built. This was bodied by Scottish Aviation as a centre-entrance 30-seat coach, complete with toilet, and was used on Anglo-Scottish services for a few years before being returned to Albion and serving as staff transport until the mid-1960s.

Singularly unsuccessful

Single-deckers from Albion were singularly unsuccessful in finding fleet business in Scotland

Left: Glasgow was obviously a target customer for Albion, and it received one of the only two KP71 underfloor-engined chassis built. The 39-seat two-door bodywork was by Prestwick-based Scottish Aviation. No BS1 ran for Glasgow from 1952 to 1959, when it was returned to Albion. Roy Marshall

Below left: Western SMT was the other postwar Venturer customer in Scotland, taking 16 CX37S with lowbridge Alexander bodywork that owed something to contemporary Leyland designs. John Aldridge

after the war. Not that they had done particularly well in the immediate prewar days either. The key models were the Valkyrie, Valiant and Victor, the last-named a lighter-weight model.

The two key Valkyrie models were the CX9 with a 6.6-litre four-cylinder engine, and the more common CX13 which shared the CX19 Venturer's 9.1-litre unit. It was in effect the continuation of a prewar design, introduced in 1937, as indeed was its CX19 double-deck counterpart.

The Valiant CX39 was in effect a replacement for the CX13 Valkyrie, introduced in 1948 and featuring the bigger engine already seen in the CX37 Venturer.

Below: Western also took the other Albion KP71 chassis, which had a Scottish Aviation centre-entrance coach body for Glasgow-London services. It is seen in Ayr bus station during its three-year stay with Western. It was thought to be still essentially an Albion demonstrator at this time.
G. W. Morant

The light Victor had a straight frame and was initially offered in 1947 with an 80bhp 4.26-litre six-cylinder petrol engine, as the FT3AB, before being joined in 1948 by the FT39 with a four-cylinder 75bhp Albion diesel unit of 4.88-litre capacity.

In 1950 Alexander took five petrol-engined Victors with Strachan coach bodies. These survived until 1964 which was quite a remarkable innings for non-standard petrol-powered buses in a predominantly diesel-engined fleet, but the other SMT group companies shied clear of Albion's front-engined single-deckers, apart from a pair of Valiants operated by Western.

They did find a fair number of smaller buyers though. John Carmichael's Highland Bus Service — which despite its name was based near the mining town of Glenboig and served nowhere more romantic than Coatbridge — bought a few new Valkyries and built up a fair fleet of used ones. Macrae & Dick in Inverness had a few, while even further north, the Sutherland Transport & Trading Co ran a fleet of Victors.

Indeed the Victor coach was quite a popular choice for small fleets, combining rugged reliability with reasonably low maintenance costs. It was almost Scotland's answer to the Bedford OB…

Takeover by Leyland

The takeover by Leyland brought changes at Scotstoun. The Venturer double-decker, which wasn't selling anyway, was axed. It's doubtful if many people noticed. The Valkyrie and the Valiant had been rendered obsolete by the new

Below: One of two Valkyrie CX9 supplied in 1948 to Macrae & Dick, Inverness, with Brockhouse bodywork. The buses passed to the newly-formed Highland Omnibuses in 1952 with the Macrae & Dick business and No A111 is seen at Farraline Park bus station in Inverness.
Ian Maclean

Below: Another Valkyrie, this time with a 1950 example with much-rebuilt Walker bodywork in the fleet of Simpson of Rosehearty, is seen in Aberdeen's Mealmarket Street bus stance in the mid-1950s.
Roy Marshall

Right: This 1955 Victor FT39 with Strachan bodywork was used by Lowland Motorways for its service linking St Enoch Square in Glasgow with Renfrew Airport.
Roy Marshall

Below: Alexanders took six of these Nimbus NS3Ls in 1960 with stylish Alexander 29-seat coach bodies for use on extended tours to the north of Scotland. Two were transferred to Highland Omnibuses in 1965, but the rest lasted with Alexander (Midland) until 1970.
Stewart J. Brown

generation of underfloor-engined chassis being sold in increasingly large numbers by Leyland and its main rival, AEC. So they too vanished. Which left the light-duty Victor flying the flag, and filling a gap at the bottom end of Leyland's passenger range.

But that wasn't the end. If there was a market for a 31-seater in the Victor class, why shouldn't it have the benefits of an underfloor engine? Thus appeared the Nimbus MR9 in 1955, built by Albion and powered by a 3.88-litre four-cylinder version of the O.350 engine used in Leyland's lightweight Tiger Cub.

One Scottish operator, Alexander, took 15, eight of which were allocated to the associated David Lawson business in Kirkintilloch. These had

Above: An Albion demonstrator was this 1964 VT21L Victor with Duple Firefly coach bodywork.
Stewart J. Brown

29-seat Alexander coach bodies and were used on holiday coach tours to the Highlands, where weight and size restrictions on single-track roads precluded the use of full-size coaches. A few were bought by other Scottish operators — most notably Highland Omnibuses and Wiles of Port Seton. Some were exported to England. Later Nimbuses featured 4.1-litre engines based on the bigger Leyland O.375 unit and were coded NS3. Production ceased in 1963.

A slightly more successful Leyland-inspired model was the Aberdonian, developed as a cut-price Tiger Cub. It used the same engine as the Tiger Cub, but in a chassis which weighed almost a ton less. The name was designed to indicate frugality, one of the traits attributed to the good burghers of Aberdeen.

Again Alexander was a major user, ultimately taking 22 — although it would seem fair to suggest that these must have been at the expense of Tiger Cub sales — so the Albion plant's gain, slight as it was, was Leyland's loss. Western SMT took three. Scottish Omnibuses in Edinburgh had one. So did Edinburgh Corporation Transport. These were all bodied by Alexander.

The Aberdonian was also fitted with bodywork by Plaxton, which widened its appeal amongst small operators. But few were sold. It was discontinued in 1960.

Serious attempt

A marginally more successful coach was the new VT-series Victor with vertical Leyland O.350 (and later O.370) engine. This marked a serious attempt by Leyland to challenge Bedford's pre-eminence in the light-weight coach business. Both Duple and Plaxton offered bodywork, but again real sales volumes were elusive. The best-known Scottish user was Hutchison's Coaches of Overtown.

Next for the Scottish market came a new double-decker. The Albion Lowlander was in effect a lowheight Leyland Titan PD3. The Scottish Bus Group, which during the late 1950s was dividing its double-deck orders between Bristol Lodekkas and Titans with lowbridge bodywork, had decided that the days of the side-gangway lowbridge body were over. It wanted a Lodekka-equivalent from its other major supplier.

Which isn't quite what it got. The Lodekka had been designed from the outset as a lowheight bus and had a low-set driving position. The starting point for the Lowlander was Leyland's existing Titan which meant a high driving position which, in turn, created problems for bodybuilders. Alexander in particular made a meal of it, with an untidy seating arrangement around the upper deck front.

But whatever the compromises, the Lowlander sold in healthy numbers to SBG, with Western SMT, Central SMT and the three Alexander companies between them taking 194 over four years from 1962, making this compromise design Albion's best-selling postwar 'decker in its home market. If SBG had been expecting Titan standards of reliability, it was doomed to disappointment. Lowlander deliveries were slow, the buses introduced semi-automatic gearboxes to those fleets taking them, and they soon developed a reputation for unreliability.

Central SMT's were transferred to Highland Omnibuses and Alexander Fife, after just three years in service. Western, too, was quick to dispose of some of its vehicles. All Lowlanders had 9.8-litre Leyland O.600 engines and while most were LR1s with Pneumocyclic gearboxes, there was a manual option available in the LR3.

Rear air suspension was offered on the LR5 (semi-automatic) and LR7 (Manual) models.

First Viking

The last Albion bus chassis to be sold in its native country was the Viking. The first Viking took to the road in 1964, a demonstrator running in the livery of Alexander Midland. It had a vertical Leyland O.370 engine mounted at the front, and a set-back front axle which allowed an entrance in the front overhang opposite the driver.

SBG services in rural Scotland were in the early stages of being converted to driver-only operation, and the Viking was designed to provide a low-cost light-weight rural bus to replace elderly halfcab Leyland Tigers and AEC Regals. The concept was right — as a few hundred R-series Fords in the 1970s later indicated — but the timing wasn't.

However that wasn't the end of the road for the Viking. The front-engined VK41 continued as an export model. Scottish operators were instead offered the back-to-front VK43. This had the same driveline — Leyland engine (now the uprated 400) and Albion constant-mesh gearbox — but mounted in the rear overhang.

In SBG terms the Viking was in effect a replacement for the Leyland Tiger Cub. That it carried one passenger fewer — 40 instead of 41 — in a slightly longer body, is indicative of the problems inherent in using an in-line vertical rear engine, which wasted a lot of space at the rear of the saloon. Long mechanical linkages to connect gear lever to gear box, some 30ft away, could also be a challenge for some drivers.

The first of the new-generation Vikings entered service in 1965. The last arrived in 1970, by which

Below: The Lowlander was Albion's best-selling postwar home market double-decker, and the Scottish Bus Group companies were the main customers. This Central SMT LR1 model with Northern Counties body, new in 1962, was transferred to Alexander (Fife) only three years later.
Stewart J. Brown

Above: The Albion Aberdonian was effectively a cut-price Leyland Tiger Cub. This 1958 example had an Alexander 41-seat coach body. A similarly-bodied AEC Reliance follows it.
Stewart J. Brown Collection

time there were 228 in SBG service including one VK49 with Pneumocyclic gearbox. The three Alexander companies were the main buyers, but small numbers were bought by Central SMT and Scottish Omnibuses. The only other Viking supplied new to a Scottish operator, went to Clyde Coast Services. It had a stylish body by Park Royal, which was also part of the Leyland empire and signalled yet another unsuccessful attempt by Leyland to break into the light coach market.

Small operators in the private sector a number of small bus and coach operators added Albions to their fleets, particularly in the early postwar years.

And while sales to what later became known as third world countries remained reasonably healthy, elsewhere in the

Below: Dodds of Troon specified full-fronted Duple A type bodywork for three of these 1949 Valiant CX39N.
Roy Marshall

Above: Albion's last home-market bus model was the Viking, and again Scottish Bus Group companies were major customers. This 1967 Alexander (Midland) VK43 example has Alexander Y-type bodywork of the general style fitted to all SBG Vikings.
Stewart J. Brown collection

United Kingdom postwar Albion buses were pretty rare. The only major user was the Red & White group, which added both Venturers and Valkyries to its English and Welsh fleets until its sale to the British Transport Commission.

And so with the rear-engined Viking, Albion's time as a supplier of Scottish-built buses to Scottish operators, ended. It did continue, in time-honoured tradition, to supply rugged front-engined models to operators in Africa. But chassis production at Scotstoun came to an end in 1980, when manufacture of the export-only Clydesdale and Viking models was transferred to the former BMC truck factory in Bathgate.

Scottish major operators — the Scottish Bus Group companies and the municipal fleets bought a total of almost 650 buses from Albion after the war, spread over a period of some 25 years. But the bulk of their business went to the other builders — Leyland, AEC, Daimler and, to a lesser extent, Guy. Small operators too, tended to put most of their business with the bigger manufacturers including, of course, Bedford.

The Leyland take-over in 1951 clearly sealed Albion's fate, but its role as a supplier of buses to Scottish operators was already in decline.

Stewart J. Brown has been involved in the bus industry for 30 years. He has worked for the Scottish Bus Group, United Transport Overseas and Leyland Bus. He has also spent periods as a professional transport journalist, working for Bus & Coach and Motor Transport. He now runs a marketing and public relations consultancy, specialising in transport.

Left: The Marlow suspension bridge over the River Thames posed operating problems for Thames Valley. A combination of narrow archways and a strict 5ton weight limit necessitated lightweight vehicles — and even then buses were only allowed to carry 15 passengers across the bridge, any over that number had to walk across and rejoin the bus on the other side! Over the years special batches of vehicles for the route linking Marlow with Maidenhead have included Karriers, Leyland Cubs, Bedford OBs and Bristol SCs. In 1970 some Bristol SUS4As, with four-cylinder Albion engines, were purchased secondhand. Seen here on 25 June 1970 is No 196, which originated with Western National. P. R. Wallis

Below: This monument to the Duke of Wellington stands outside the main gates to Stratfield Saye House, in north Hampshire. The estate was purchased by Parliament in 1817 and given to the Iron Duke as an expression of the nation's gratitude for its deliverance from Napoleon. Just over 150 years later, on 21 March 1971, Weymann-bodied Dennis Loline III, No 491, of Aldershot & District passes by on service 12 linking Aldershot with Reading, a joint operation with Thames Valley. Wellington Monument was a timing point on that service as well as on Thames Valley's service 6 between Reading and Basingstoke. A number of scheduled short-workings on the 6 terminated at Wellington Monument, the stop being just visible to the right of the picture. P. R. Wallis

SECOND FIDDLE/3